My Luke and I

My Luke
and I

Eleanor Gehrig ~~and~~
~~Joseph Durso~~

Thomas Y. Crowell Company
New York   Established 1834

Designed by Ingrid Beckman

Manufactured in the United States of America

Library of Congress Cataloging in Publication Data

Gehrig, Eleanor.
    My Luke and I.

    1. Gehrig, Lou, 1903–1941.   2. Gehrig, Eleanor.
3. Baseball.   I. Durso, Joseph, joint author.
II. Title.
GV865.G4G44   796.357′092′4   75-44457
ISBN 0-690-01109-1

    2   3   4   5   6   7   8   9   10

To Dr. Caldwell Esselstyn
for his devotion to Lou and me

E.G.

Contents

And early though the laurel grows
It withers quicker than the rose.

—A. E. Housman,
"A Shropshire Lad"

Prelude

~

Paradise

T HE *2,141 islands of Micronesia are scattered across the West-*
ern Pacific like emeralds carelessly flung over the sea. All are sce-
nic, most are lush, but fewer than 100 are inhabited. They are
strung in three chains—the Carolines, Marshalls and Marianas—
and all three were mauled during the naval battles of World War
II. But since then, despite the tourist traffic searching for the sun,
they have regained the languor of life in the tropics.

If you gathered the islands together into one cluster, they would
form a "land mass" about half the size of Rhode Island, in an
ocean area as broad as the continental United States. And the
most prominent edge of the cluster would be Guam: a strange and
strategic dot in history from its discovery by Magellan in 1521 to
the B-52 bombers that recently lifted from its runways for Viet-
nam, more than 2,600 miles away.

It is a green place 30 miles long and 4 to 8 miles wide, a volcanic island 5,800 miles west of San Francisco and 1,500 south of Tokyo. A rather flat place with mountains along the south side "rising" to just 1,334 feet at a kind of summit. Below are fertile valleys stocked with rice, coconuts, coffee, tobacco, pineapples, broad-leafed banana trees, breadfruit and ironwood trees, small pines, sword grass and, along the white beaches, rubber trees in thickets.

For six months of the year, northeast trade winds caress the island; then, between June and November, the rain season arrives, with an occasional typhoon lashing the landscape. But the temperature averages eighty degrees or so around the calendar, with the sun reflecting a startling range of colors from the sea, jade within the protective reef that surrounds the island, turquoise in the middle depths and solid blue or even purple beyond.

To the geographers, and even to some philosophers, it sits in the sun like a remote Paradise, isolated from most of the afflictions of the outside world. One report after the war portrayed it this way:

"Guam is listed as a 'clean' port by the Navy, with no venereal disease, malaria or dengue. One strange disease is present—amyotrophic lateral sclerosis. Lou Gehrig's disease.

"Although it strikes only Guamanians in the population, the incidence in a couple of villages at the south of the island is the highest known. Neither cause nor cure has been found. . . ."

1

My Iron Man

THE 21 Club in New York is an oasis of sorts on Fifty-second Street between Fifth and Sixth avenues, and we always sat upstairs for lunch in those days. I was there one afternoon in June, 1939, and I didn't have too many complaints. I was thirty-four years old, I was married to a great-looking, successful and faithful man, and I had half a dozen years of happy memories behind me. I wasn't too troubled by the news that Europe was barreling into a war, and I had never heard of anything called amyotrophic lateral sclerosis.

For almost a year, though, I had been hearing of a lot of other things—because my great-looking, successful, faithful husband supposedly was suffering from one or all of them. It was like playing Russian roulette. One doctor said he had a gallbladder condition. I suspected it was a brain tumor. Other people voted for old age; at thirty-six, Lou Gehrig was just past his peak.

This was no ordinary man we were fussing over, either emotionally or physically. Sensitive, but not demonstrative, a huge but proper wallflower, maybe shy, maybe even square. Kind of an adult Eagle Scout, a six-footer with strength, stamina and an unreal threshold of pain. A professional athlete for more than fifteen years, and one of the elite of the proud New York Yankees for 2,130 games in a row. *In a row.*

In one game, he hit 4 home runs in Philadelphia and just missed hitting a fifth. One year, he led both major leagues in everything: batting average, runs batted in and home runs, which is nice work if you can get it. Another year, he knocked in 174 runs; the next, 184. And I don't know how many times he went to bat with the bases loaded, but I do know that twenty-three times he unloaded them.

The trouble started in 1938, when his batting average slipped 56 points to .295. Lou still batted in 107 runs and hit 29 home runs that year, and though I'm no statistician I still realized that was a drop of 20 home runs in two seasons—and nobody touched off any skyrockets. He was in a "slump," so they just looked the other way. Then, that winter, there were times when he stumbled over curbstones, and maybe *I* looked the other way. When we went ice-skating, Lou started to fall down more than usual, too. And at home, he began to drop things, as though he'd lost some of his reflexes. He was in a *slump?*

Gallbladder, the doctor said, so okay—gallbladder, it was. If you're his wife, you settle for that, especially if you remember all the times he'd been hit on the head by pitched baseballs. But never in a million years could I blame his gallbladder for the sad new sight of this giant person—my "Iron Man of Baseball"—missing the curb or dropping a kitchen cup.

After a while, even Lou began to get the idea that something was missing. He didn't drink much except for a couple of beers, but our little guessing-game must have started to get to him after the Yankees had taken four straight from the Chicago Cubs and swept the World Series. We were at the team's victory bash at the Commodore Hotel, and one of the other players came over to me during the evening and said: "You'd better look after Lou. He's drinking triples, and he's really bombed."

So now it was eight months later, and Lou had gone through all the motions. He worked out in the gym all winter. He rented a house near Huggins Field in St. Petersburg, Florida, so he could be closer to the training camp in the spring. He exercised on rollers to strengthen his legs after each day's workout. He got 4 singles in 28 times at bat in the first 8 games of the regular season back north, and then benched himself, ending his "streak" at 2,130 games in a row. One day he even lost a bout with a ketchup bottle. He couldn't work the top off, and finally just handed it over to his teammate Bill Dickey without a murmur.

After quitting the lineup, Lou retreated to the dugout and watched during that May and early June, appearing only to carry the lineup card to home plate before games and present it to the umpires in place of the manager, Joe McCarthy. Then back to his ringside seat while grown men played a child's game and, like a child, he peered with envy while they did it. And by then everybody was looking the other way.

Upstairs at "21," I called to the waiter and asked for a telephone. He brought an extension phone and plugged it in at the table where I was sitting with Fanny Barrow, the wife of Edward G. Barrow, who had been running the Yankees since he followed Babe Ruth to New York from the Boston Red Sox eighteen years earlier. Another friend of mine, Anna Hartman, and her husband had also contributed to the Great Debate about Lou's condition. The husband, Lou Hartman, was a business associate of Ted O'Leary, who in turn was a partner of Joseph P. Kennedy in the Haig and Haig Scotch organization. O'Leary had a brother, Dr. Paul O'Leary, at the Mayo Clinic, and the Hartmans had been saying that we should stop fooling around and send Lou to some place like Mayo to find out what was wrong with him.

Anna reminded me that she had a good contact there and, rather than waste any more time, I should call them and get started. So, just like that, I picked up the extension phone and called Rochester, Minnesota.

I'll tell you, it's not exactly like calling your family doctor to make an appointment for a routine checkup. I was making a long-distance call to people I didn't know, except by reputation as the most distinguished medical detectives in the country, maybe the world, and it had nothing to do with a routine checkup.

When the call was put through, I discovered one thing right away: Lou Gehrig's name, and maybe even Lou Gehrig's troubles, were no secret in the medical world. Dr. O'Leary quickly switched me to Dr. Charles Mayo himself, and I got to the point fast: I suspected that my husband was suffering from a brain tumor. Dr. Mayo didn't comment on that, but he agreed it sounded serious, whatever it was, and he said: "We'll welcome him with open arms. Get him here."

That, I figured, was easier said than done. But I sweated out that particular problem all afternoon while the Yankees were playing the Chicago White Sox in my old hometown. Then at seven o'clock that evening, knowing that the game was over and Lou would be back in his room, I picked up the phone in our home in Larchmont and called the Del Prado Hotel, where the Yankees stayed in Chicago. There was nothing routine about this call, either; it was like none of the thousands of other calls I had made during all the years when I calculated time by the ebb and flow of the baseball schedule—two weeks at home, two weeks on the road, one week home, one week away.

For more than a month, since Lou had left the lineup on May 2, those conversations had been skipping over the hits, runs and errors, anyway. This time, I got right to the point even faster. I simply asked Lou if he'd do me a favor.

The voice at the other end was the same. Even the greeting was the same—he always called me "pal," sort of man to man. But even for an agreeable guy like Lou, the willingness to comply was total, no questions asked. I suppose that no questions had to be asked, after six sweet years of sharing good times and one terrible year of sharing a fear that was growing into a kind of unspoken panic. Would he do me a favor? Just like that. And, just like that, he answered: "Yes, pal."

I delivered the favor. I said I'd arranged for him to fly from Chicago to the Mayo Clinic, where Dr. Charles Mayo was waiting for him. The doctor had promised to keep everything private, had promised anonymity, in fact. I told Lou to get out of Chicago as fast as he could. Maybe Lou was unusually docile, maybe he was unusually beat; maybe he was just unusually sick and knew it. Whatever the reason, this time he just replied: "Okay, pal." And my "favor" was granted.

I made another call that day—that day, looking back on it, was when I stopped fretting in a vague way and started full-time trying to track down this new "thing" in my life. I called the doctor in New York who had been treating Lou for the last year. He was a distinguished doctor, though I didn't ever believe that his line of reasoning was particularly distinguished in this case: He still thought we were talking about a gallbladder condition.

I told him that I wanted him to know what I'd been up to—that I'd told Lou to go to the Mayo Clinic and that he'd agreed. There was bound to be some public fuss, probably even headlines before we were done, and I was saying in effect: Doctor, brace yourself. You know, two or three of our mutual friends were patients of his, and I didn't want him to be embarrassed. I was really trying to give the man a chance to protect himself when the story broke. At least, he could say that he personally had referred Lou to another doctor at Mayo. But he didn't get, or at least he didn't accept, the point.

"You're a very foolish young lady," was the way he phrased it. He might've been piqued because I had decided to change course, and that would have been a human enough reaction. He might've been convinced that I was reaching for straws. He might've been convinced that he was on the right track himself. I'm not sure exactly what he thought. He even intimated that the Mayo Clinic wasn't what it was cracked up to be, any more. But he didn't budge—and neither did I.

The next morning, Lou went to Joe McCarthy, told him about our decision and flew to Mayo. By then, I had already been back on the hot line to Dr. Mayo. I never was the type of woman you'd call a shrinking violet, and now I was hitting people for favors on all sides.

"My God," I said, as though I was finally aware of the enormity of my own aggressiveness, "he's agreed to come. Do me a favor. When you make the diagnosis, call me—don't tell Lou."

"Are you sure?" Dr. Mayo asked, and I guess he was trying to be firm and easy at the same time. "It's the policy of the Mayo Clinic to tell the facts to the head of the house."

"I've got news for you," I said. "*I'm* the head of the house."

This wasn't Eleanor Twitchell just keeping a stiff upper lip. This was Twitchell sticking close to the relationship

that Lou had created when he tossed our checkbook over
to me after the wedding with the remark: "Our old age is
in your hands."

He meant it, too. He even bought me a typewriter and
set me up in business: secretary-treasurer of the family accounts, answering the mail, buying the insurance, even in-
vesting the money. The anointed brain. The girl guide of
Chicago—Hyde Park High School, St. Xavier's convent
day school, horseback riding, fast motor cars, afternoons
on the golf course, regular visits to the racetrack. Keeper
of the keys to my father's business—a co-op apartment
house without tenants. Director of personnel for Saks,
Chicago, when the Depression struck, leaving the director
in charge of firing instead of hiring the personnel. Secretary to the construction engineer at the Century of Progress.

And now, head of Lou Gehrig's troubled house.

The first staff man who watched Lou's arrival at the
Mayo Clinic was Dr. Harold C. Habein, the chief diag-
nostician, who was waiting for him in the lobby and who
gave him the big official greeting. It was the first time Dr.
Habein had ever seen Lou, and he formed a fast conclusion in the first thirty seconds after observing the celebrated captain of the New York Yankees walk across the
lobby. He noted the shuffling gait and the overall expression, shook hands, then said: "Excuse me a minute, Lou."

To Harold Habein, the impression was unmistakable
and devastating. He had watched his own mother die
slowly with the same shuffling gait, the same staring ex-

pression, and he went straight inside to Dr. Mayo's private office and said: "My God, the boy's got amyotrophic lateral sclerosis."

It was a surmise, not a diagnosis, but nothing that happened in the next two years changed its accuracy by one shred. A day later, I telephoned the clinic again from Larchmont and Dr. Charles Mayo got right to the point, or almost to the point. "We think it's serious," he said. "We'll put him through the six-day tests—and hope to God that we're wrong."

They put Lou with the other transient patients in the hotel across the street from the main building of the clinic, and every day I would call the clinic office before calling the hotel. For six days, the doctors measured every part of his health that was measurable while I waited and worried and prayed back home. We had always had a promise between us—he wouldn't keep playing baseball past the age of thirty-five or thirty-six. We had enough money, we had enough insurance, our parents were healthy.

"Don't wait till they take the bat out of your hands"— that was the deal. They called me with the diagnosis on June 19, his thirty-sixth birthday.

The call came from Dr. Mayo and Dr. O'Leary, and it hit me amidships. "Take your time and give me the works," Lou had ordered them with a laugh when the testing began. And they took their time and gave him the works. At the outside, they told me on the telephone, he had two and a half years to live.

They also kept their arrangement with me, the head of

the house, and told Lou something less than the full truth. It ran something along the lines of the statement that Dr. Habein prepared for the public:

"This is to certify that Mr. Lou Gehrig has been under examination at the Mayo Clinic from June 13 to June 19, inclusive.

"After a careful and complete examination, it was found that he is suffering from amyotrophic lateral sclerosis. This type of illness involves the motor pathways and cells of the central nervous system and, in lay terms, is known as a form of chronic poliomyelitis—infantile paralysis.

"The nature of this trouble makes it such that Mr. Gehrig will be unable to continue his active participation as a baseball player, inasmuch as it is advisable that he conserve his muscular energy. He could, however, continue in some executive capacity."

In a way, I think, Lou was relieved by the findings, though he was given no idea of the full consequences. For one thing, it proved to him that he was not just an aging player slowed by time, but the innocent victim of a disease that disintegrated his muscles and destroyed his speed and power. It was no bargain, except in those narrow terms that spare any performer his pride even if he is spared nothing else. He also was convinced that his body would do whatever his spirit willed, even though his body would soon drain that towering spirit.

What he suspected beyond that, who knows? On the surface, he might have known some of the medical facts I knew: Many years ago, it was called "creeping paralysis," and its victims were kept in attics or other hideouts, be-

cause they were considered to be idiots. The disease is
thought by some medical men to be hereditary, but it can
skip a couple of generations. It can be carried in generations from, say, Europe to America, or Asia. Doctors
don't always diagnose it correctly, though after the Mayo
report on Lou they took a survey and listed 250,000
cases, and now in the tank towns and other places, they
call it simply Lou Gehrig's disease.

Whatever he knew, a few days later Lou took a pencil
and wrote a letter to me in his clean, beautiful script and
told me the doctors had decided it was something called
lateral sclerosis, but not to worry. He did not know that I
already knew; he just wanted to protect me, as far as possible, from what *he* knew:

Mornin' Sweet:
  Really, I don't know how to start and I'm not much at
breaking news gently. But am going to write it as there is
no use in keeping you in suspense. I'll tell it all, just as it is.
  As for breaking this news to the papers, I thought and
the Dr.'s approved, that they write a medical report and
then a laymen's interpretation underneath and I would tell
the papermen here that I felt it was my duty to my em-
ployers that they have firsthand information and that I felt
sure they would give it to the newspapermen. That seemed
the most logical way to all of us here and I felt it was such
vital news that it wouldn't be fair to have Joe and Ed read
about it in the papers.
  However, don't be too alarmed or sympathetic, for the
most important thing for me is no fatigue and no strain or
major worries. The bad news is "lateral sclerosis," in our
language chronic infantile paralysis. There isn't any cure,
the best they can hope is to check it at the point it is now

and there is a 50–50 chance for that. My instructions and my physicians will be furnished me by Dr. O'Leary.

There are very few of these cases. It is probably caused by some germ. However, my first question was transmission. No danger whatever. Never heard of transmitting it to mates. If there were (and I made them doubly assure me) you certainly would never have been allowed within 100 feet of me.

There is a 50–50 chance of keeping me as I am. I may need a cane in 10 or 15 years. Playing is out of the question and Paul suggests a coaching job or job in the office or writing. I made him honestly assure me that it will not affect me mentally.

They seem to think I'll get along all right if I can reconcile myself to this condition, which I have done but only after they assured me there is no danger of transmission and that I will not become mentally unbalanced and thereby become a burden on your hands for life.

I adore you, sweetheart.

2

Tristan and Isolde

The "mystery" of Lou Gehrig was not exactly solved by the gloomy but scientific report from the Mayo Clinic. If anything, it was deepened as the word was thrust at the public in headlines—much bigger, much blacker, much starker than that handwritten letter that had thrust it at me.

Some people speculated that he had "caught something" during the All Stars' long trip to the Orient a few years earlier. Others thought it just as clearly, and just as intriguingly, had been prompted by the strain of his endurance streak: 2,130 baseball games in a row. One newspaper even suggested that he had been stricken with a form of infantile paralysis, that it was communicable and that a

kind of panic was gripping the team because it had fallen
into a slump on the field just as mysterious as Lou's sad,
sensational illness. They had marveled for thirteen years
at his sublime strength; now they were marveling at his
stunning weakness.

My own problem was not to find answers for their questions, but to find them for myself—to find the cool, calm
mask that he would be seeing every day and to make certain that it would never reflect the torment behind it. For
six years together, I'd been Eleanor the easy rider and
sunny soul who thrived alongside his solid, solemn stance
in the spotlight. Now I was handed a new role and a new
secret: to subdue what was hounding me so that it could
not begin hounding him.

You don't get too much warning for something like that.
I got exactly three days, in fact, to learn the role, to master it and to carry it off. Three days—because the doctors
at Mayo held him over for three days after their diagnosis.
It was ironic: They passed that extraordinary sentence on
him, then begged him to stay for a few days for an ordinary *encore*—a little fishing in one of the 10,000 lakes of
Minnesota. They realized that fishing was one of the joys
of his life and, with one of those personal little touches in
the midst of all that science, they realized that fishing with
Lou Gehrig was one of the joys of their life. So the doctors got hold of a boat and headed for the lake, fishing for
a few days and half-sharing the secret that was wracking
me a thousand miles away back home.

Lou did it because he was alreay reconciled to the half
of the secret that he shared: a 50–50 chance to stay alive
and maybe a cane in fifteen years.

So they went fishing while I had three days for a grim fishing expedition of my own—for the answers that might prop me up for my own role when he finally flew back. I went straight to a specialist in New York and pumped him for all the known details of amyotrophic lateral sclerosis. The doctor seemed stunned by it all, but he leveled with me though he managed to skirt the grisly part of it. He also got me a pass to the library of the New York Academy of Medicine at Fifth Avenue and 103rd Street, near Central Park, and I burrowed into the bookshelves and files and found my answers.

I cried all the way home from the library with my new knowledge, and it took me two days to get the crying out of my system for my new role and the new "front" that went with it.

Lou flew home from his fishing and I was waiting at the airport in Newark. I drove the Packard and met him—alone. Nobody else was there, just the two of us, together again for the first time since he had headed West with the Yankees fretting over his .143 battting average and the four singles he'd scrounged in his final eight games, four singles that sounded no echoes of the 2,717 other hits that had gone before. Just the two of us, and we played it up beautifully, laughing for no reason all the way home. No tears, no brooding now and no declarations that "You'll be all right, Buddy."

We had recently moved from New Rochelle to Larchmont, and we drove there chattering and close. I was putting up my front, it was that simple and that sad. And then I was starting to draw a conspiracy of silence around my house and around the doomed man inside it.

One of the first things that happened after we reached home and began piecing things together was that the world started beating a path to the door. Like a jack-in-the-box, Mayor Fiorello LaGuardia of New York came up with a job offer. He telephoned and said he wanted to see Lou, and even made an appointment for the next day. I never spoke privately to the mayor about Lou's condition. It was a "neck-down" disease, and I felt that as long as Lou still had his mental faculties, it wasn't too crucial for LaGuardia to know the whole "truth." But the mayor was a sharp person who sensed the imponderables in the situation, so I did work out a side deal with him—I would tell him when Lou's judgment or strength began to wane.

I called LaGuardia to establish that deal and said: "Mr. Mayor, I don't want to shock you"—but he interrupted and said quickly: "I know, I know." So I just added: "You can take my word that I'll let you know when I think his judgment's not right."

LaGuardia was a courtly little man who waved away the fussy details of things, and he waved away the details this time. He simply gave Lou a ten-year appointment as one of the city's three commissioners of parole, saying the only immediate problem was that there was a law requiring city officials to live within the five boroughs of New York City. So I had to go on the road again and find a new place for us to live inside the city limits.

I picked out a house in Riverdale, the "country" section of the Bronx alongside the Hudson River near the northern tip of Manhattan Island. It was a house that had some ramps in it, and a garage on the incline so that you could enter through the back way. I knew that one day Lou would be in a wheelchair. It was a beautiful house on Delafield Avenue and, before long, it began to fill up with neighbors like John Kieran and with droves of people from the downtown worlds of baseball and the stage.

It took a lot of acting to pull it off. Everybody who came to the house was screened and warned: no backslapping or stuff like that because Lou was too smart for that. It was an act, and I had to act out the lead role.

Lou and I both had figured that we came from broken families, so we had made this pact never to lie to each other, never to go through that scene. But now I told him that I had read up on "it," which was true enough. But I didn't tell him what I'd learned. So I was really telling him the big lie. I just lied all the way through, and he believed it—so trustingly that he didn't read up on it himself or crowd his doctors to tell him more.

The day we moved into the house in Riverdale, a few months after he had come home from Mayo, he was still walking; he needed some help, but he was groping along. It was a white house with pheasants walking on the lawn and lots of trees throughout the streets nearby. I hired a butler and maid who lived in, and my mother came from Chicago later and helped because I stayed awake most nights with Lou. I told him the house cost $75 a month, but actually it cost $175, which was a lot then, but—as lies went—that wasn't so monstrous.

One of the mailmen showed up that day, came bounding up, grabbed Lou and said with real delight: "God, this is great, Lou. A guy I work with tells me he has Toscanini on his route. I finally topped him."

I suppose that to him, Arturo Toscanini just swung a

baton, while the new man on *his* route swung the big bat in town. Each to his own taste.

Every day after that, I drove Lou downtown to his office on Centre Street, or to Rikers Island or the Tombs, where he would continue the transition from first baseman for the Yankees to one of LaGuardia's three commissioners of parole. Many of the prisoners were young or black or underprivileged, and some were women, and he'd see them all—rapists, hookers, pimps, addicts. It was quite a shock to his noble and somewhat innocent soul, but he took it.

Sometimes the prisoners would complain to him that "I got a bad break." Then I would always nonchalantly light his cigarette and place it in his mouth and take it out again after a puff while he listened with both hands on the desk because after a time he couldn't lift them.

He'd never get riled and say, "What do you mean, you got a bad break?" The words would flash through my mind, but he never flung them out for the *coup de grâce*. He would just be silent for a moment and let the complaint hang there in the air: *bad break*.

When Lou's legs began to go, I went to LaGuardia one day and finally made the confession that I'd neglected to make earlier. The mayor was sitting in a box in Yankee Stadium, and I just came out and told him that Lou's days were numbered and it would be necessary to give him a leave of absence. I gave him a thumbnail sketch of the problem, telling him that this was the terminal phase of the disease and I wanted to prepare him.

LaGuardia was horrified. He actually turned white, sitting there in broad daylight along the first-base side of the stadium. He accepted it, but he recoiled at it, the news that Lou would not be back behind the desk, listening to other people's sad stories and letting them reflect on his own. I could remember, not so long before, when the mayor was briefing Lou for the job and telling him: "Don't let anybody touch you"— meaning that it was a job where everybody tried to get to you. A job where he wound up touching everybody else.

Back home, the "conspiracy" went on after we had stopped our drives downtown every day to Rikers Island and the Tombs. It thickened actually into a phenomenal charade, played out by bright and talented people who filled the driveway with their cars and filled the house with their own "thing." We turned it into an "open house" that I was running nonstop. I set up an open bar, even though none of the pack drank very much for some reason, and we had a buffet spread out almost every night when the performances started.

Many comedians and show people came to the house, almost as though it was another stop on the summer circuit. Fred Fisher, the songwriter, came almost every day—and he knew what was happening, but he kept it surrounded by the music he had written: "Dardanella" and "Peg o' My Heart" and "Ireland Must Be Heaven." There was Pitzy Katz, an old vaudevillian, who did make it every day. We'd met them both through Billy Rolfe, a dress manufacturer who knew Lou and who dragged these two characters around to keep things moving after he'd learned about Lou's illness.

John Kieran, who wrote the sports column for the *New York Times* and who amazed people with his encyclopedic mind on the "Information, Please" radio program, lived down the street. He knew Shakespeare the way other people knew the alphabet, he could recite epic poems for hours, he prowled around the museums of the country during trips with baseball teams, and he was a bird-watcher, besides. He'd go out at five or six o'clock in the morning to spot them and watch them, and he could do it because Riverdale was country then. He'd go over to Van Cortlandt Park, too, and inspect things. Along the way, he would stop by the house and sit with Lou for an hour or so, and it was great. It was strange, though, that after we realized from the radio show what a brain he was, I started to feel uneasy around John. He seemed too smart for words, and it spoiled some of the fun to sit in the presence of all that brainpower.

You might say we developed wall-to-wall talent there, chuckles all day and all evening, and the only rule was "lights out" at eleven. Our guests were all good ad-libbers, and most of them made their living and their reputation by their wits, not by manufactured jokes. And they must have saved their best lines for those floor shows they staged every evening in the living room in front of the audience of one man in a big easy chair.

Some of the baseball people were also part of the conspiracy. Fanny and Ed Barrow knew, and Bill Dickey and Frank Crosetti—the catcher and shortstop on the Yankees—knew. Not the gory details, but they knew he couldn't make it. They knew because they had been close to him, and Dickey, who'd been Lou's roommate on the road, had been one of the first to detect the little clues that hinted at something more grim than just a slump by just another power-hitting ballplayer.

Somebody else who "knew" was Dr. Caldwell Esselstyn, who lived two blocks from us in Riverdale. He had been designated by the Mayo Clinic to come by every day and care for Lou. They had a "new treatment" then—injections of Vitamin E—and Mayo sent a box of vials to us, and Dr. Essy came every morning and went through the ritual.

Essy had been a great football star at Yale, and he came from a long line of people at Yale, so he and "Columbia Lou" hit it off well from the beginning. The Esselstyns were original Dutch settlers of the Hudson Valley, tall and straight and good-looking types. When he went to college, his father didn't let on particularly that he was a wealthy man, and he made Essy work his way through— waiting on tables at Yale. Later, all of his own children became doctors, and he eventually settled back into practice on the ancestral acres up the Hudson River. And, thirty-five years after he entered our house to treat Lou, he—suddenly, silently and uncomplainingly—was fighting cancer.

On the Fourth of July that first year, not long after Lou had come home to me from the Mayo Clinic, somebody else joined the conspiracy. It was the day that the Yankees held their "day" for Lou at Yankee Stadium, and he acknowledged the cheers and the tears with a short but moving reply of his own over the public-address system and radio. I don't know how many persons were listening that day, but it was during intermission time at the matinee shows along Broadway and one of those listening was Tallulah Bankhead. She was doing the show *The Little Foxes*, and she caught Lou's speech on the radio.

She even delayed the curtain for the next act until it was over, and then sat down and wrote him a letter. I guess you'd call it a fan letter. We started to correspond, and later Tallulah wrote and said she'd be appearing in summer theater in White Plains. I invited her over to the house, and met her at Ben Riley's restaurant. It was a well-known place, with its frogs legs and all, and Tallulah showed up with the whole troupe from the show.

I had to make a couple of trips in the car from the restaurant to the house to get the whole troupe over to Delafield Avenue, but they really raised the roof when they got there. They put on practically the entire show in our living room. They cued one another in—"take this," "cut that"—and they did all the big lines. It was terrific. There was only one person in the audience, as usual: front row, center. Did he like it? He "lost his mind."

You may have read or heard a lot of gossip about Talullah, but none of it came to the surface during the performances she created in our living room. She had made a vow at the beginning of the war in Europe that summer that she wouldn't take a drink until the war was over, and she never did—at least not in my house. And she never did an off-color line or gag, either. She "knew," too; and she entered our little scheme like a religious fanatic.

Later, the cast went on tour with *The Little Foxes* and,

whenever they came back to town, Tallulah would pop over to the house every three or four days and keep things jumping.

Tallulah was always being treated for ulcers or some other damned thing. So I told her to go to the Mayo Clinic, and I even set it up for her. She only spent two days there because they were playing a theater at Rochester, Minnesota, but she gave them two days they never forgot. She bought out the theater and spread the tickets around the hospital and around the town. There's a great line in the show—she says, "And you know how doctors are." And she gave it that great throaty laugh of hers, and brought the house down. Never tell me anything unfavorable about Tallulah Bankhead.

Not all of Lou's associations with stage stars were uplifting, though. One of them—probably the most meaningful of his life—brought him a gathering sense of foreboding, and it kept gathering around him during those months in Riverdale when our open house became an open theater. It is difficult to put into words without sounding heavy or contrived, but it was there almost from the first moment when I introduced him to the world of the arts and, especially, the opera.

When we first met, we were very different persons. I was sort of an extrovert; he was sort of an introvert. I tended to be outward-going; he tended to be more private. I acted sure of myself in social situations; he acted shy and reserved. I had been "around," in a manner of speaking, though I'd always been "around" on a short leash on a straight path; but he had had almost no contact with the

world outside his family's matriarchal circle and the
railroad schedule of the New York Yankees. He was solid
and dignified and all man; but he was—well, untutored as
far as "culture" went. But he was eager to learn.

One of the things he had never had any contact with
was grand opera, so early in our marriage I made sure that
we began to spend a lot of our winter evenings at the Metropolitan Opera House. And he took to it not only fully
but emotionally. This was especially true of the Wagnerian operas, because he could speak and follow German
fluently, so that none of the dramatic effect was lost on
him.

One season we saw *Tristan und Isolde*, all seven times it
was presented. Kirsten Flagstad sang the lead, and we got
to know her and the other singers like Lauritz Melchior. A
new world of feeling opened for Lou, a world that struck
him as not so far removed from the cheering crowds and
loud displays of the ball park where he spent his summers.

Tristan is tragic from start to finish, and you hear doom
in the overture itself. I don't say that Lou identified heroi-
cally with the majestic figure of the knight Tristan, nor
did he say that he related me to the bittersweet role of
the tortured loved-one, Isolde. But he did come away,
each time, with a growing premonition.

He was shaken by it, shaken to tears, sitting there in the
opera house alongside me. And when he got into it, into
the implications of it—the lovers who found their way
together too late in this world and maybe only in death—
he was destroyed emotionally. When Tristan lies mortally
wounded on his couch and when Tristan and Isolde sing

their final duet, Lou was besieged by fears and doubts about his own life.

I think it went back to the hard path that took Lou toward me. He had a struggling childhood, with a sick father and a domineering mother, and encountered one hurdle after another. Then there he was; suddenly grown, handsome and successful. He had the girl of his dreams, and he had a life of his own. And he also had a premonition of his own—that it couldn't last, that it was a tantalizing trick of some kind, never really meant to be. When they gave him the news at Mayo, he must have thought, "Christ, here it comes."

Lou used to go backstage at the opera and talk to Kirsten Flagstad about the story. He didn't dwell on it with me particularly—the doom part of it—but he was shaken physically, and that was long before he lay dying on his own couch.

In the earlier years, the quick years, when he wouldn't talk to me for two or three days after a slight spat, I learned later that he'd been brooding. But it turned out that he'd been mad at himself, not at me. He was so totally straight, and I was the dash of spice in his life. And that was the reason this premonition hung over him, I think. Even in the happy time—maybe *especially* in the happy time—he wasn't sure he'd ever make it. . . .

3

No. 1994 Second Avenue

IN 1903, the year Lou Gehrig was born, the Wright brothers were testing their new-fangled flying rig on the dunes at Kitty Hawk, and the United States was turning into the new century with some longing looks back at the one it had just survived. And no wonder. People often can glance *back* at the known inconveniences of life—even the known dangers of life—with some assurance or relief that things can be managed.

When you start to relive events of the past, you have a tendency to screen out the really brutal moments. When I was a kid, I can remember reading history as though it was one long and dramatic narrative. No beginning, no ending; just a stage and a lot of actors dashing around it.

Years after something happened—say, Custer's Last Stand—they used to dramatize it all nice and neat and colorful. Glorify it, as if the general had won a great victory.

At Sheridan, Wyoming, they even used to re-enact the Last Stand on the Fourth of July. It had happened twenty-seven years before, but they'd revive the "heroic Seventh Cavalry" surprised by 1,500 Crows and Cheyennes in "hideous warpaint who swooped down upon the 200 men from Fort McKenzie and surrounded, cut down and annihilated them in the presence of thousands of spectators." At least, that's the way one account of it read, and never mind that General Custer didn't play his real last stand "in the presence of thousands of spectators."

The psychology worked even for events not quite as lethal as the Little Big Horn. The year before Lou was born, John McGraw appeared in his first baseball game in New York as manager of the Giants. You've got to remember that John McGraw was hated in those days like few out-of-towners (even like few Cheyennes, I guess). He was the man who had invented, developed, perfected and *used* the old Baltimore Orioles' brand of "inside baseball" against anybody who dared to cross his path. But as soon as he switched sides and cities early in the century, he was welcomed to Broadway like a hero.

"John McGraw and his Baltimore recruits made their local debut before nearly 10,000 people," according to an account in the *New York Evening World* that I read later. And the *Times* reported that "New York's baseball team played its first game at the Polo Grounds yesterday under the new management of John McGraw. With the new management and the infusion of new blood, the New Yorks played much better ball than they had been doing. They did not win, but the home players lost the game by only one run and *put up a good article of the game.*" Whatever that meant.

When people looked ahead, though, into the murky future—that's when they would start dodging phantoms. The *Times* in those days talked about "an increase of hostility toward automobiles." One farmer took a shot at a passing automobile because it was frightening his horses. In Manhattan in 1903, "automobilists" were trying to win an increase in the legal speed limit from eight miles an hour all the way up to twelve or even fifteen. But other citizens were forming vigilante committees to head off that threat to their sanity. And two years later in Winnetka, a suburb of Chicago, not far from where I was born things were getting so bad that the mayor stretched a rope across the street and began timing cars with a stopwatch.

Lou Gehrig, Eleanor Twitchell. New York, Chicago. Two cities, worlds apart. My family was comfortably poor when I was born, Lou's family was just plain poor. He was born June 19, 1903, at 1994 Second Avenue, near 102nd Street on the upper east side of Manhattan. Besides being poor the Gehrigs had another problem; they couldn't speak English at all when they migrated to America and they were still speaking German with some acquired English overtones when Lou started to grow up.

In fact, until his mother and father died, they both had heavy accents and both lapsed into German in times of stress, if that's the right word. They argued often and, when they did, they argued in German at full volume all the time.

I don't know if the Gehrigs looked back cheerfully and looked ahead fearfully, the way other people might have done. Their life was basic and there was nothing cheerful about the way they lumbered through it. And if fear grew into foreboding in Lou's mind thirty years later, this was where it all began.

His father, Henry Gehrig, was called Heinrich when he was home, which wasn't very often. He was a leaf-hammerer, a man who pounded patterns into sheets of metal, an art-metal mechanic. He earned fairly high pay, when there was work, and he even searched for it as far away as Detroit once. But Heinrich Gehrig had a greater passion for beer and pinochle, and he found both in the corner saloon. He seldom had a steady job and he left the chief burden of supporting Lou to Christina Gehrig, his wife, the strong right arm of the family.

You're probably on thin ice when you start portraying the life and times of the woman who later becomes your own mother-in-law, especially an overpowering woman like Christina Gehrig. But these aren't *my* recollections of her; they're mainly Lou's, and all his life he never fully escaped the suspicion that he was his "mother's boy," no matter how strong and silent and muscularly self-sufficient he seemed to become as his path headed in the direction of mine, 750 miles west and several light-years apart.

There was no such thing as welfare—at least, there was no practical solution like welfare—so Christina Gehrig turned to the only "trades" she knew to keep food on the table: She hired out as a cook and a domestic. She also took in washing, and one of the first things Lou remembered was helping his mother pick up and deliver the neighbors' laundry almost as soon as he could walk. She got plenty of work, too, when her cooking skill was discovered and, since their neighbors were almost as poor as the Gehrigs, she ranged farther and farther afield—cooking dinner for better-off families crosstown, taking home their dirty laundry, lugging it back clean and starched the next day with Lou carting the laundry bags and dozing off to the clang of the trolley bell whenever another passenger got aboard and deposited his nickel. When they reached home, he remembered the reward of it all: great cuts of roast beef, Christina's homemade pies and a sampling of the blue-ribbon delicacies she had prepared for the "rich folks," all snugged in between the mounds of dirty shirts and sheets.

They moved a lot in those days, depending on how much money was in the till and how much work Lou's father could manage to find in the neighborhood. Lou first began to learn English when he was five, and he began to polish it when he went to Public School 132 on 182nd Street and Wadsworth Avenue. But until he got to grammar school, Lou didn't know just how poor—and strange—he was.

They made fun of his clothes and his accent. They called him Heinie or the dumb Dutchman. Maybe they even sensed that he felt secure only with his mother. But Lou was big and tough for his age and, though he might have been "dumb" and he certainly was a "Dutchman," at least they didn't back up the nicknames by picking many fights with him. Not after the first round, anyway.

In those days, a lot of school-age children used to get up at five o'clock in the morning and play until it was time to go to school. Lou didn't particularly like it that way, especially when it came time to go to school, even though he was a good student in a stolid, German sort of way. But the playgrounds and vacant lots gradually gave him a chance to find an "out," a chance to realize that he was big and chunky and strong and fast. And particularly tough at football and soccer, games that made more sense to his father than baseball, the "American game," which the old man did not understand.

Maybe we were star-crossed lovers from the start. Even Lou's strength somehow got turned into a weakness, and he was a kid who didn't have that much going for him. Pop Gehrig belonged to a *Turnverein* and, proud of the strength of his growing son, took him to the club and showed him how to use the parallel bars, pulleys and weights. Maybe it was just Pop Gehrig's genius for doing the wrong thing. He emphasized muscle-building, and Lou worked for years building his muscles until he looked like a junior edition of Sandow, the strong man. Then he got into professional baseball and was so muscle-bound that he almost fell over his own feet.

Anyway, Lou's first brush with "something better" was connected with baseball. He was on the track team in grammar school and, as the strongest kid in the class, he also put the shot. But when Lou was twelve years old, his grade-school baseball team won the championship of the Parks Department league—and for the first time, Henry Louis Gehrig got his name in the newspaper.

By then, baseball was a big part of his life after school, and a big part in Americanizing his life after school because it was one thing that he had in common with his "American" friends. Like them, he could not only imitate the baseball heroes of the day but save them and trade them on the cigarette cards that carried pictures of Ty Cobb, Zach Wheat and Christy Mathewson. One of his favorite players was Honus Wagner, maybe because he was "the Dutchman," too. And his favorite team was not the Yankees, who were slipping from obscurity as the Highlanders into obscurity as the Yankees, but the Giants of Mr. McGraw. The Giants won the National League pennant three years in a row while Lou was in grade school and they were the toast of the town long after—until the next decade, when Lou ironically would team up with some fairly tough ball players to depose them.

On the sports field, Lou was as good as anybody and better than most. Off the field, he was terribly shy and insecure. He was afraid of his father, he loved his mother. His father's word, backed up by a Teutonic fist, was law. So Lou and his mother became allies in a kind of Resistance. Not much money, not much joy.

Pop Gehrig was not a drunken, villainous lout. He was the product of his background and his time. His sense of duty was absolute. His sense of humor was Middle European: a man slips on a banana peel and lands on his behind, that's a howl. Mom Gehrig, on the other hand, was not a heroine, even though there was something heroic in her fixation to keep the family together and to make something of her son. She had had one other child, a daughter named Sophie who died on March 27, 1906, at the age of one year eight months. Diphtheria. And now she was left with the square, blocky son.

If I'm making it sound like Oliver Twist, I've missed the point. Lou was poor, maybe he was born behind an eightball, maybe his family attachments were out of proportion. But he was neither a zombie nor a plaster saint. He loafed away a lot of hours swimming with the other kids in the Hudson River near 181st Street, or crosstown in the East River off Yorkville. He played marbles at 181st Street and Fort Washington Avenue. He hitched sleigh rides and got into snowball fights at Deep Grass Hill. He roasted stolen potatoes, "mickeys" to the insiders, in vacant lots over trash fires. His father loved him and was proud of him, though he rarely showed it. Once he even bought his son a catcher's mitt for Christmas. But that proved another of Pop Gehrig's near-misses. It was a mitt for right-handers, which most catchers are, and Lou was a left-hander, which most first basemen are.

Pop Gehrig wasn't a drunk. He loved the saloon because it was his club, a place where he could meet his friends, play pinochle, jaw about the old country and do it all in German without any patronizing or muttering remarks from the "American" workers on the job. He wasn't lazy, either, but there really wasn't much work in his trade and maybe the saloon became an escape from that reality, or from home—because, while Christina would never dare to put it that way, she didn't leave much doubt that her husband was something of a failure. I always had the feeling later that his wife and son resented the fact that he spent too much time over pinochle and beer, and he resented the fact that they were subtly allied against him.

One incident always stuck in his mind about his father's pinochle playing. Pop got lucky one night at the card table and eventually got home very late. He kept bumping around the bedroom, weaving across the floor, probably looking for some place to stash his winnings. But while he was sleeping it off the next morning, Mom stumbled onto a bonanza of seventeen crumpled dollars. And what did she do with it? She went off on a kind of sad orgy. She hustled Lou off to Coney Island and they spent the day on one mad spree of roller-coaster rides, hot dogs and ice cream. I don't think that Mom, or even Lou, would have understood why it turned me sad, almost mourning, when they'd laugh about it years later. To them, it was the most fun they had together in all the years he was going through school; to me, it was the story of that wrenching life on their own roller coaster, day in, day out.

So there they were. Lou going through grade school, his father working when he could, his mother helping out as a cook and laundry whiz. No great tableau there, except that *she* got more and more obsessed with the idea that her son wasn't going to be condemned to the same sort of hard life, and school would supply the escape. Later Lou told me that he never played hookey or missed a day through eight years of grade school, even with a mild case of pneumonia. That was his own idea, to go to school anyway, even though for some reason the thought of his slogging to school with a temperature or a cold still horrifies me.

Most boys who were Lou's age, and who were in Lou's place, never even went to high school in those days, let alone to college. But Christina bulled straight ahead. At her insistence, when he graduated from P.S. 132 he went on to the High School of Commerce instead of going out with his friends and getting his "working papers" and a job. She was *that* intent on his "making something" of himself, so much so that he even refused to go out for any sports in high school for a while. Lou was still a good student, though it came hard to him, but he was afraid to spend the time playing games when he should've been cracking books.

The Gehrigs were still dirt poor, and the nickel carfare each way was the biggest item in Lou's "budget," to use a farfetched word for it. New York's winters can be bitterly cold, too, but he never owned an overcoat, either. In the worst weather, he wore only a sweater and a muffler. But he never wore an overcoat until I put my foot down after we were married and insisted that he buy one.

This may sound like a soap opera or a Horatio Alger story: poor German kid from Yorkville grows up in dull home, wondering what it's all about, flexes his muscles and finds success and stardom. But that's like Custer's Last Stand—too simple, too cut-and-dried, not enough innuendoes and fine strokes. What I'm remembering is a kid who grew up with a great chance to become completely mixed-up, muscles and all. Shy, embarrassed that he didn't have any clothes or any money to treat anybody to an occasional soft drink or cone. Heinie, the Dutchman, the kid who "spoke funny." And, by 1917, one of the "dirty Huns" who had sunk the *Lusitania* while everybody else's father was getting ready to march off to hang the Kaiser.

The Gehrigs moved from Yorkville, but that was like running out into the open, away from the camouflage of the old neighborhood. Now Lou wasn't just another squarehead, but *the* squarehead. Not just another Dutchman, but *the* Dutchman. No place to hide now, just take it like a man, like any man of fourteen.

If there *was* any soap-opera side to Lou's story, it began to take shape when he finally started to get into school sports. The high school freshmen lined up on the practice field for soccer, and Lou would boot the ball almost the full length of the field. The coach asked him to try out for the team, but his mother wouldn't give her permission, for one thing. Then Lou convinced her it wouldn't get in the way of his precious schoolwork, and she relented. He made the team as a halfback and Commerce High won three winter championships in a row.

Lou still was embarrassed by the war, and he still kept his head down most of the time, bearing down on his bookkeeping course for some distant and probably un-known goal. College, maybe; sharing his mother's dream that he would somehow go to college, and through college, and then become an engineer—even though the dream was vague in everybody's mind.

Then his father took sick, and the Gehrigs suddenly had another ordeal to go through. He was so sick that he couldn't even work, not even when a job turned up, so Christina Gehrig had to decide who *would* go to work to keep things together: she or her teen-aged son. She won the toss, so to speak, and answered an ad for a cook-housekeeper at the Phi Delta Theta fraternity house at Columbia University. And after her husband recovered enough to do some sort of work, she got him into the same fraternity house as a handyman and janitor.

This might have been one of those blessings in disguise, now that I look back on it the way Lou described things. They'd all get up early—Lou to take the subway or "El" to the High School of Commerce, his mother and father to go crosstown to Columbia. She still took in washing on the side, and Lou was running errands for the neighborhood grocer and butcher shops after school. The family was finally pulling in the same direction.

Lou even chipped in, part-time, at the fraternity house and for the first time started earning a dollar in sports. He sometimes earned $5 at a clip playing baseball. He was now six feet tall and 200 pounds, and he had plenty of semipro teams around Manhattan to get involved with, even though he was still a seventeen year old in Commerce High. They'd play on Sunday against teams from other New York neighborhoods or from New Jersey: $35 guaranteed to each team, with $5 for the pitcher. So Lou Gehrig became a pitcher.

One of his classmates was Lincoln Werden, who later became a sportswriter for the *New York Times*. They were classmates in high school as well as college, and years later Linc Werden wrote some impressions of his friend:

"But then, who was Gehrig? One of thousands of the city's youngsters who poured into the gray buildings daily, whose parents like those of the rest of us were hardworking, struggling folk hoping their sons some day might become businessmen. Lou attended the High School of Commerce on West Sixty-fifth Street. It had no spacious playgrounds, no trees or grassy lawns. His early training included playing ball on a backyard, walled-in campus whose ground consisted of lumps of cinders. Any resemblance to the turf of the Yankee Stadium was purely accidental.

"He came to school by subway or the 'El,' took two steps at a time going up and down stairs, seldom wore a vest or top-coat in cold weather and had a terrific appetite. What made us suddenly realize at Commerce that Lou was different from other varsity ball players was a home run that he hit in an inter-city game against Lane Tech of Chicago at Wrigley Field. Before that, if you happened to play in a class game against him and he knocked the ball over your head, you just ran after it. I know you didn't console yourself by saying, that's the future Gehrig of the Yankees. You were simply glad when he wasn't at bat."

It was in 1921, and he came home from school to tell his parents that the Commerce High baseball team was

There I was in Chicago, a growing young woman watching all sorts of people playing games. . . . I went from the more or less sheltered sidelines of the good life into the sporting and social circles that surrounded it, and somewhere during that transition I met Lou Gehrig. . . .

There he was in New York, kicking footballs and socking baseballs, a grown man making a name for himself playing games . . . and there may have been no greater contrast in a time of contrast than the one involving me and the squarely-built, squarely-oriented baseball player who became the man of all my lives.

ABOVE at Commerce High, New York.

BELOW at Columbia, 1923.

GEHRIG
1ST BASE

The New York Yankees gave him $1,000 as a bonus . . . so he was going to be a professional ball player instead of a distinguished engineer . . . and when school ended that June, he reported to the Yankees and their musclemen—Ruth, Bob Meusel and all the others in their gleaming new stadium across the river in the Bronx. (Culver Pictures, Inc.)

43

going to Chicago. Commerce had won the city championship and the ball team was being treated to a trip to the
moon—a trip to Chicago to play the champions there,
Lane Tech High. It wasn't easy. It took the intervention
of the coach plus assurance that he would deliver Lou back
home safe and sound before Lou's mother would give her
permission. And then he was off for his first train trip,
first Pullman ride, first night in a hotel, first meal in a
hotel dining room, first night away from that troubled, almost tortured, family circle.

I have two huge scrapbooks before me now, half a century later. They are so huge that I have to open them on
the floor to get a good look. Mrs. Gehrig used to stuff
Lou's early newspaper clippings into a drawer, and it took
me almost a year to straighten them out. The first book
that I patched together opens with the newspaper story of
that ball game in Chicago, all yellowed and dried now
with a headline that reads: "Louis Gehrig Hits Ninth-Inn-
ing Homer With Bases Loaded."

There wasn't anything in the headline about his pitching, probably because the final score was untidy: 12 to 6
in favor of Commerce. But there was a lot of surging language about Lou's hitting, even in the solid old *New York
Times*, which started it like this:

"Chicago's champions went down to defeat by a score of

That was some baseball team. Babe Ruth batted No. 3 in the lineup
with Gehrig batting No. 4. They were some pair. Between them, in
1927, they knocked 107 baseballs over fences and knocked in 339 runs.
This was the postwar "Golden Age" of sports. . . .

12 to 6 in a game laden with thrills and heroic acts and featured by a home run over the right-field wall by Louis Gehrig, the New York lad known as the 'Babe Ruth' of the high schools. The real Babe never poled one more thrilling, for the bases were filled, two were out and it was the ninth inning."

It didn't actually win the game, though, even if the legends since then imply that it did. But it was strong enough stuff to merit a "play by play" account of all nine innings in the *Times*, as though the World Series had been at stake. The infield star for Lane was a boy named Freddie Lindstrom, who played shortstop then and who later played third base for the New York Giants. But when Commerce cranked up the bats in the ninth, Freddie got buried along with everybody else.

"Ninth: Pfleger took third base for Lane and Christman took center field in his place. Starke went out, Stevenson to Ryrholm. Troy singled to center and went to third when Christman let the ball go through his legs. Troy failed to touch second base and was thrown out, Christmas to Pasquinelli. Jacobs walked. Bunora was safe on Pfleger's fumble. Johnson walked, filling the bases. Gehrig fulfilled his advertised name of Babe Ruth by driving the ball over the right-field wall for a homer, clearing the bases. His teammates gathered around the plate and greeted him with handshakes when he crossed the plate."

Babe Ruth? The strong boy of Baltimore and of Boston, traded to the Yankees in 1920 and now, a year later, firmly established as the strong boy of New York: 54 home runs in his first year, 59 in his second, when Lou was a senior at Commerce. Already, Ruth was leading the Yankees in their attack against John McGraw's grip on Broadway, and no fooling about it. The Yankees were still sharing the Polo Grounds with McGraw's Giants because they had no stadium of their own, but they were suddenly beginning to outgrow the role of "subtenant" and to out-flank McGraw and his entrenched team. The year before they ransomed Ruth from the Red Sox, the Yankees played before 619,162 fans. Then Ruth began hitting baseballs over the fences, and they played before 1,289,422, more than double their previous attendance—and 100,000 more than the Giants drew.

And that was when Mr. McGraw got on his high horse and raged one of his famous rages to Charles Stoneham, the owner of the Giants: "The Yankees will have to build a park in Queens or some other out-of-the-way place. Let them go away and wither on the vine."

So back in 1921, when the newspapers were calling Lou "the Babe Ruth of the high schools," they were trotting out their superlatives. Unreal, probably; but superlatives anyway, in those roaring accounts of that nine-inning game between Lane and Commerce, replete with school-boy errors, kids who forgot to touch second base, too many walks, eighteen runs in one game, and a grand-slam homer over the Wrigley Field wall by the big pitcher from New York.

The Commerce team headed home on the Twentieth Century Limited and arrived at Grand Central at 11:15 the next morning. They were met by a crowd of 5,000 persons who had waited an hour and a half, and then the whole bunch stepped out smart as anything for Commerce High, marching in a daze behind the Hebrew Orphan Asylum band, up Park Avenue from the terminal.

At Fifty-ninth Street, seventeen blocks north, they were all reviewed by the Board of Education, which then joined the parade for the rest of the march to the school at Sixty-fifth Street. Into the school auditorium, snaking down the aisles, finally seated while the superintendent of schools, Dr. Ettinger, gave the speech of the day, relating the experiences of the team in "wild and woolly Chicago."

In my outsized scrapbook, photos cover the entire back page of the *Daily News*, which had sponsored the trip and which was going to town over the result. There is one picture of the team in an open-air bus, the boys leaning out the windows and holding a big sign that someone in the crowd had brought along, reading: "Welcome Home From the Wild and Woolly."

I was fifteen at the time, going on sixteen. And I was untouched by all the commotion and all the headlines, untouched by "the Babe Ruth of the high schools" who was provoking both the commotion *and* the headlines. I was still safe from the agony and the ecstasy of those huge scrapbooks, building my own memories without knowing that I was on a collision course with him, back there in my own wild and woolly Chicago.

4

My Kind of Town

I⸏ may have seemed wild and woolly to Dr. Ettinger and the boys of the High School of Commerce varsity baseball team, but to me it was awkward, lively, exciting and growing fast. Chicago, "my kind of town." The town that Carl Sandburg put to verse and Fred Fisher put to music.

I was born there in 1905, and the place has haunted me with memories ever since. Echoes, too. Even years later when Lou and I were living in Riverdale and our house had become a camping ground for missionary-entertainers. People such as Fred Fisher. Songwriters are horrible piano players, except maybe Gershwin, and Fred Fisher stood clearly in the majority. There he was one evening, pounding my carved, black grand piano as though it were a tom-tom.

"You sound like a player in a whorehouse," I told him, probably giving him the benefit of the doubt.

"I was," he replied, not missing a beat. "In the Everleigh house in Chicago."

That toddlin' town, Chicago, a world removed from the grim gray Yorkville neighborhood where Lou was struggling along, back in his town. So I had a Chicago background and a New York future. I had—as John F. Kennedy gibed years later when he received an honorary degree from Yale to top off his Harvard education—the best of both possible worlds.

Both my parents were of Irish descent. My father, Frank Bradford Twitchell, said he could trace his "line" back to the first governor of Massachusetts, which may be the reason the headlines later said Lou Gehrig had married a "society girl." But by 1933, the only society we Twitchells belonged to was the human race because, with the Depression, we were as broke as everybody else.

My mother was a Mulvaney, and there was a boat in her past, too. The boat that took her ancestors to this country in the great wave of Irish immigration after the potato famine of 1848, when they left home in droves rather than starve to death in droves, as many did. Well, *she* had a claim, too: a descendant of kings. And after her death, while I was a guest in Dromoland Castle in Killarney, I stealthily planted a small tree on the grounds to supply some "roots" to her claim.

So my mother and father, without the comfort of any kings or governors, met and married in Chicago. A pair of orphans, actually, and for the first few years of their marriage also a pair of wandering nomads, moving around the United States following the horses. That's right, following the horses.

It sounds great, but they didn't do it because they were the idle rich. They did it to keep from remaining the idle poor. It was a job, and a good job provided by my father's uncle Gene Austin, one of the best of a breed: price makers, specialists whose talents were highly prized by the bookmakers from Illinois to Texas.

Price makers filled a great social need in those days, though maybe "social" isn't the right word. It was long before the payoff prices at race tracks were set automatically by computers tied into the parimutuel machines. Instead, the payoff prices were fixed by the price makers— the men who decided the odds in races according to the breeding of the horses, their past performances, the records of the jockeys and the ability (and the honesty) of the trainers.

The bookmakers, who operated under the sanction of the racetrack, were legitimate and highly respected businessmen. They changed the odds according to how much money was bet on the different horses, but it was the price makers who calculated the fairest "opening line" that set up the betting equation for both the bookmakers and their gambling public.

My father was Uncle Gene's favorite relative, so when he needed an assistant he gravitated to Dad and kept the job in the family. And my father leaped at it because it had all the elements: travel, excitement and more money than the $6 a week that grocery clerks and bank tellers fetched at the turn of the century.

Frank Twitchell was a dapper, charming sort who had been an altar boy once but who hadn't let the experience handicap him later. My mother was a tiny, pert redhead who had been raised in a convent and housed by an assortment of Chicago cousins. They met at a race meeting in Chicago, and it was love at first sight. In fact, he was the only love of her life and, years later, she would drag me to all the Tyrone Power movies to stare at the "dead ringer" for my father from their racetrack days.

They were Catholic, though not terribly devout, probably because he became too exposed to the "other worldliness" of the sporting crowd while she had lived religion night and day in the convent. Besides those Tyrone Power looks and smooth manners, he had another quality that impressed her; he didn't drink anything stronger than beer. That was to come much later.

I was still a toddler when they started to hit the road with Uncle Gene, chasing the horses and the seasons. The only thing I remember from those earliest times was "drilling" with the soldiers at Fort Sam Houston in San Antonio during our gypsy days. I was only three years old, my mother told me later, but I already was picking up some tricks—I did my drilling with the foot soldiers but raised my sights to the officers on their payday, wheedling some small silver for some big candy.

The "road" had its moments, but it also had dirty day coaches and rundown boardinghouses. And when my mother became pregnant again when I was about five, one of my parents decided to blow the whistle. Maybe he decided, maybe she demanded, I don't know. But they settled down in Chicago, and I started growing up in an apartment at Sixty-first and Ingleside Avenue on the South Side where my brother was born. My next stop was the public grammar school across the street from a Jewish orphanage, and now the onetime racetrack brat was nestling into the mid-South Side of 1910.

It was a sprawling desert of middle-class Chicagoans, with only a couple of cases of money—the old George M. Pullman mansion near Lake Michigan and the rows of imposing houses along Grand and Michigan boulevards. West of us was the desolate "working section," known for years as "back of the yards," where thousands of Irishmen made a living by sloshing around in the gore of the stockyards, protected by hip boots and bent on raising God-fearing families of boys to become cops or lawyers, though sometimes producing gangsters instead; or girls to become the mothers of second-generation judges, priests and politicians. To the north stood the mansions of the new packing and industrial millionaires, safely removed from the smell of the stockyards. And to the south, the steel mills churning out fire and sooty smoke all day and all night.

We were in the middle, in geography and in cash; between the stinking rich and the working poor. We were the comfortable poor. We didn't bicker, we didn't bitch and we were beholden to neither the rich nor the rest of the poor.

I suppose we yanked ourselves up to being just plain

"comfortable" when my father got a job as manager of the Heidelberg Café, one of the better known restaurants in town. My mother was pleased, even proud, but the switch in fortune just annoyed me because it made my father a late sleeper. I'd come home from school and have to wheel my baby brother around the neighborhood while my mother kept house, did the washing and baked the bread, and while my father was still sleeping. We couldn't disturb him because he'd come home from the restaurant in the middle of the night. Then, by the time I had wheeled my brother in, headed for the playground and finally returned for supper—my father had gone back to work again.

We were fed and put to bed and, if the wind was from the west, the scent of the stockyards would come drifting in. I can still remember the highly advertised "fresh lake breezes." They were an event, though, since they showed up only when the wind was blowing from the east. Otherwise, we were trapped between the stockyards and the steel mills.

When I graduated from grammar school, the girls were expected to make their own white middy blouses and skirts, but I can still remember how my mother bailed me out of that chore by doing it herself, the way she bailed me out of other chores later. This was during World War I, about the time we took another step up the old ladder, moving to a better neighborhood called South Shore, and things began to happen.

What happened was that Chicago was a city of parks and, although I didn't know it then, Chicago's 5,000 acres of parks were to play a major role in my life. In those days, before World War I, the city's park commissioners weren't politicians but prominent and usually civic-minded businessmen. The park system was split into two parts, with the bigger bloc on the South Side. Jackson Park, larger even than Central Park in New York, had been the main site of the World's Fair in 1893 and, when I was a girl, it still had many of the big, old ornate buildings from a quarter of a century earlier.

Jackson Park wasn't a bad thing to have in your backyard, but there was a rub—the park commissioners for the South Side weren't happy with the concessions. The concessionaire's agreement with the city was about to run out, and the commissioners had already decided not to renew it. They used to go to the Heidelberg to eat, before or after their meetings, and they got to know and like my father. They'd even ask his opinion; after all, he was running one of the best restaurants in town. And so, one thing led to another, and the commissioners wound up asking my father if he would take over the park concessions.

As corrupt as the city administration was to become later—and, for all I know, as corrupt as it may have been then—there was no hint of any payoff or graft. At least, none that I ever got wind of. The commissioners apparently were out to hustle better food and service in the South Park system, and Frank Twitchell more or less fell into place.

I doubt that my father had a hundred dollars in the bank at the time. His chief assets were his brains and his imagination. But he borrowed enough money to get started, and suddenly he had more responsibility—and we all had more of the material things of life—than ever before. But that was the story of our life: By the time our roads crossed, I was snug and safe in a warm family cocoon while Lou was toughing things out. Whatever we were, and whatever we became, started with that study in contrasts.

You flash back on things and you revive the impressions that were part of your mood or general feeling when you were a kid. One thing—I was a loner, something like Lou, but I was healthy and happy and busy. I had a shoebox full of marbles that I'd won, I could ice-skate on the rinks that dotted every school playground in the winter and, even though Chicago has one of the roughest climates in the world, I never remember feeling cold in winter or too hot in summer. I had it made.

My father had it made, too. The first thing he did was to arrange to buy hot dogs made to his specifications from Oscar Mayer, the meat packer. How's that for class: hot dogs *made to his specifications*. My father built a better hot dog and people started beating a path to the parks, where his hot-dog stands began to sprout in strategic places along the South Park Lake Front. So don't tell me that life doesn't take us on some strange twists and turns.

There was a beautiful golf course in Jackson Park, too, and the next thing my father did was to refurbish the old ramshackle buildings—they formed a kind of municipal clubhouse—and he renamed them the Golf Shelter. No liquor, just shelter and plenty of food. He also put up this thing, sort of a glorified gazebo, close to the ninth hole where the golfers could stoke up in the middle of a round. He called the shots, all right. The Golf Shelter became one of the "in" eating places in town, and families who didn't know the difference between a sand trap and a mousetrap started to crowd it from May to September, weekdays and weekends.

The old German Pavilion from the 1893 Fair was still standing in Jackson Park, and my father made that one a diamond in the rough, too, calling it the Bathing Pavilion. Twitchell & Co. began to live high on the hog.

No wonder Fred Fisher later admitted to me that his musical career had been nourished behind the velvet drapes there: It was an accomplishment, just as it was for a talented Jewish songwriter to spin out tunes like "Peg o' My Heart."

There's no scrapbook to preserve my home runs and field goals half a century ago, just a few photographs that show me riding the crest of the wave of prosperity generated by my father's big splash. In the winter, I'd skip the dinky rinks of the playgrounds and head for Jackson Park and its enormous flooded ponds and the enormous hot chocolates produced at rinkside, courtesy of the concessionaire himself. In the summer, I got into golf—not so great on the short game, but fairly great off the tee for a kid, and I didn't mind hamming it up, either.

Later I grew horse-crazy and spent hours on the bridle path of "my father's parks." He even got hold of an ex-jockey whom he'd staked to a job in one of the stables, and then I had myself a horse teacher, too: elbows in, back straight, knees tight, English style all the way. And a horse named Black Cloud, the best in the stable, and you guessed it—I "nagged" my father long and hard enough, and Black Cloud was mine.

I wasn't a tomboy, even with all the sports activity. But the dainty little-girl outfits and the dainty little-girl conversations of my schoolmates struck me as a waste of time. I probably threw my mother into a bit of a panic, not being frilly and all that. She even bought me a life-sized doll with china-blue eyes in a porcelain face, blonde hair, diapers and a whole wardrobe of outfits that I was supposed to change. But except for a few times when I'd go through a "doll number" for my mother's benefit, I never really figured that any doll measured up to any 7-iron, putter, skating pond or galloping horse. I wasn't even too thrilled over her orders to "watch Frank" or "take the baby for a walk" or later to "take Bud with you to the park"— even though my baby brother seemed a cut above any other doll-sized thing around the house.

Just a good life, and in those years before the war we had the good outlook to go with it. I didn't know about "poor little Belgium" and didn't care particularly about the Czar or the Battle of the Marne later. To me, the main event was the big show down at the Palace or the Majestic every Monday when the new vaudeville bills came in. I remember Sophie Tucker, Savoy and Brennan, Georgie Jessel calling his Mama on the telephone, Will Rogers twirling the lariat. I don't think I ever *paid* to see them all on the stage. You just sort of milled around the exits at the end of the show when everybody was coming out, waited a minute until they turned down the house lights and then slipped into the nearest empty seat.

After I graduated from grade school, my parents sent me to Hyde Park High, and the thing I liked best about that was it was right across the street from Jackson Park. Acres and acres of room to roam around in and, sure enough, I began to run up a better attendance record at Jackson Park than at Hyde Park.

They tried to counter that little problem by switching me over to St. Xavier's. I guess the idea was that the good sisters could do a few things with me in the convent day school. But algebra and geometry didn't improve either with age or geography, so I cut out of there, too. And if twenty-one days in a row is the truancy record in the Convent League, then I set it.

The arrival of those "hot" new automobiles didn't help, either. My father bought a Stearns Knight, a status symbol as significant as a Cadillac and almost in a class with a Locomobile or a Pierce Arrow. I didn't need any prompting, but I got it anyway from the weekly chapter of *The Perils of Pauline* at the old nickelodeon, where Pearl White zipped around as cleverly as Barney Oldfield or Eddie Rickenbacker. The temptations were great. Later on, Dad bought a donkey-brown, air-cooled Franklin that was in a class by itself. It never boiled over in the summer and always started in the winter. We nicknamed it "Maude" and we went first-class on wheels with that great invention.

The good life took a few jolts, though, when President Wilson sent the American Expeditionary Force under

General Black Jack Pershing to save the world for democracy. I was only twelve then, but I remember the headlines in the *Chicago Tribune* when the Doughboys beat the Huns at Château-Thierry and Saint-Mihiel. Robert R. McCormick owned the *Tribune*, and he was Over There as a colonel in the A.E.F., a fact he didn't let Chicago forget for the next forty years.

I also remember that the heavy German population in the city came under a cloud, the way the Gehrigs' German circle did in New York at the same time. German names, even German breweries, suddenly became targets. In restaurants, "hamburgers" became "liberty steaks" for a while, and the Heidelberg became the Woodlawn Café. And Bertha Schmidt became Betty Smith.

I didn't appreciate it then, but things were changing fantastically in just those few years when I was growing up. When my parents got married, the only people who owned automobiles were either rich or nuts about sports. The only women who painted their faces with rouge and lipstick were "loose." But by the time the war ended in 1918, the automobile was running wild on the landscape and so was rouge and lipstick. Some women even smoked cigarettes—at home—although that was still considered "fast," and it took guts or a European background for a lady to smoke in an exclusive restaurant. For that matter, Irene Castle broke tradition just by bobbing her hair. They were even talking about giving women "the vote," that's how far things had charged along.

When the war ended, the next step in "progress" became the Noble Experiment of Prohibition, which caused a revolution in the cities, especially Chicago. And the out-break of peace also caused a revolution in our otherwise safe and sane family.

It happened one Sunday at breakfast when my father picked up the *Tribune*, glanced at it and turned pale. He stacked the paper under his arm and literally ran out of the house. About an hour later, a messenger boy showed up with a large manila envelope addressed to Mrs. Frank Twitchell, who opened it, found a copy of the newspaper inside, spread it across the dining-room table—and then *she* turned pale. She also broke into hysterical tears as she read through the note inside.

She was still shaking when I picked up the paper and saw the headline: "Marine Returns to Find Wife Loves Another." It was a haymaker, all right. A young marine had returned from Over There to find that his wife had been having a red-hot love affair with her boss, Frank Twitchell, the prominent concessionaire of the Chicago park system. An "alienation" suit soon followed.

It was bad enough to have my snug illusions wiped out like that, and a family scandal plastered across the Sunday *Tribune*. But what hurt even more was that my father hadn't had the courage to stay and face the music. It was his note to my mother that had set her off, announcing and denying it all in the same explosive bundle, protesting that it was some sort of blackmail plot. I know she wanted desperately to believe him, and when he phoned to see if he could come home, he was received with open arms over a tear-stained but suspicious face.

I was still just a kid, just into my teens, but it was the

end of my age of innocence. My father swore that whatever there had been between him and the marine's wife
had ended. But neither my mother nor I believed him.
Looking back on it, I think my mother made a terrible
mistake, but I suppose she wanted to know for sure because she reacted in a disastrous way. She started to check
up on him, shadowing him in the Stearns Knight—with
me at the wheel, young as I was, because I already could
out-drive her. And she finally found what she'd been
searching for.

Apartments then were cheap and easy to get, especially
for somebody with my father's income. So once he recovered from his Sunday-morning remorse, he began to move
his girl friend to new lodgings every few weeks, with my
mother and me on his footsteps. One night we followed him
to a new place, and it turned grotesque. Mother sent me
up the fire escape while she rang the front bell.

I was perched outside the bedroom of the apartment
when all hell broke loose at the front door. My father
opened the bedroom window to beat a diplomatic re-
treat—only to stare into the wide-open eyes of his daughter.

Handsome, kindly, considerate—to me, he'd been all of
those things. Now I was fourteen and none of those things
saved my illusions. I was devastated, and amazed. The
Other Woman wasn't even a sultry Nita Naldi; just a
skinny tart in a negligee, and nowhere near my mother in
sheer looks. She was the front-runner of a whole series of
disillusions that crowded me over the next few years. My

father, my well-loved father—was just another guy with other flaws.

My parents patched things together "for the sake of the children." My mother still kept house, cooked, sewed, did his shirts, fed his children, all the things that are supposed to be done for the sake of each other. And he bought her a roadster.

He even opened charge accounts for her all over Chicago and hired a maid. We had a beautiful apartment, three cars and plenty of cash. On the surface, a happy and prospering family headed into the decade after the war; beneath the surface, a grieving and poor family headed for its own state of siege.

I think now that the happiest time of my life until I married fourteen years later was before Dad became so successful—so "successful"—when I was still a believing kid and the Twitchells were still comfortably poor. Long before Lou Gehrig came to town with the baseball team from Commerce High and hit his famous home run over the ivy-covered wall of Wrigley Field into the streets of wild and woolly Chicago.

5

Tale of Two Cities

In the 1920s, the United States began to slide from the tensions of the great war in Europe into the roaring decade of wonderful nonsense, a time of suffragettes, heroes, heavyweights and hoopla.

It was a time when Johnny finally came marching home, when actors like Ethel and John Barrymore were bringing a touch of family class to the stage while new motion pictures like *The Queen of Sheba* were bringing a touch of chariot action to the silver screen. A time of public idols like Jack Dempsey, Douglas Fairbanks and Suzanne Lenglen, and even of animal idols like Man o' War. You could wheel around the countryside in spiffy new automobiles like the Chandler roadster or the Amesbury Berlin sedan, or you could soar across the Continent in new biplanes from Paris to Brussels to Amsterdam in only four and a half hours, "one-third of the time formerly required by railway."

You could read of the latest scientific report from Madame Curie, the latest "reparations" report from the chancelleries of the world capitals or the latest battle report involving John McGraw and his New York Giants. You could do anything after a while but buy a drink—legally.

"The vandals sacking Rome," observed Gene Fowler, "were ten times as kindly as the spendthrift hordes on Broadway. The Wall Street delirium was reaching the pink-elephant stage. Chambermaids and counter-hoppers had the J. P. Morgan complex. America had the swelled head, and the brand of tourists that went to Europe became ambassadors of ill will. World War I killed nearly everything that was old Broadway. Prohibition, the mock-turtle soup of purists, provided the *coup de grâce.*"

It was a wide-eyed, wide-open time when people passed unenforceable laws to control the nonsense—and then just as cheerfully found ways to make certain that the new laws wouldn't control anybody's nonsense. For a time, the "rum courts" that had been set up to fortify Prohibition were nearly as busy as the speakeasies that had been set up to fortify people against Prohibition. And the celebrated criminal lawyer William J. Fallon, once summoned to a huddle before the bar of justice in court, was asked by the judge if he had been drinking and replied with absolute charm: "If Your Honor's sense of justice is as good as his sense of smell, my client need have no worry in this court."

Along the way, the government figured that the public was spending something like $10 million a day for bootleg whiskey. One reason, suggested the police chief in Chicago, was that "60 per cent of my policemen are in the bootleg business." And even Al Capone, who presided over the mess as the tyrant of the underworld, complained that "there's one thing worse than a crook, and that's a crooked man in a big political job."

When the decade started, I was a fifteen-year-old girl, and when it ended, I was a twenty-five-year-old woman. In between, I went from the more or less sheltered sidelines of the good life into the sporting and social circles that surrounded it, and somewhere during that transition I met Lou Gehrig. And there may have been no greater contrast in a time of contrast than the one involving me and the squarely built, squarely oriented baseball player who became the man of all my lives.

I'm not saying, thinking back on how it happened, that I was ahead of my time and he was behind his time. It was just that we took almost opposite routes to reach the same point, the point where we got together and started traveling the *same* way for the few years that we did share. There he was in New York, kicking footballs and socking baseballs, a grown young man making a name for himself playing games; there I was in Chicago, a growing young woman watching all sorts of people playing games.

By then, I was also the dedicated truant from the best schools money could buy; and Lou was the dedicated student taking the long step from high school to college. At least, it was long in those days, but the step was shortened for him because of his well-known muscles. He already had attracted a lot of attention from colleges while he was playing baseball and football at Commerce High, and he was mulling over some offers of financial help when the football coach at Columbia University got a look at him in action.

Columbia was practically in the Gehrigs' backyard, but it was out of their reach as far as money went. Still, Lou's mother had been working there at the Phi Delta Theta house, scrimping for his education, and Lou had even joined her there for a while waiting on tables. So, with a little nudge from the director of athletics, Lou entered the Extension Department at Columbia to get enough academic credits so that he could become a full-time freshman a year later—and a full-time athlete, as well.

"At Baker Field, where Columbia University's football squad is training," Burris Jenkins wrote in the *Evening World*, "a football volleyed up from the 10-yard line yesterday afternoon with a deep 'plunk.' It rose in a long, high spiral and, just before it descended, the seemingly tiny pigskin wavered, then whirled itself through the air like a projectile in a long slant to the ground, gaining remarkable forward distance as it went. It dropped just over the 30-yard line of the opposite goal."

Scrapbook or no scrapbook, that still strikes me as a lot of fairly rich phrasing to describe a practice punt. But that's the way it was, nice and snug inside the make-believe world of the campus and its afternoon games. And Burris Jenkins was only warming up.

"The punt," he went on, giving it the old college try,

"was over 60 yards long. It was made in the face of quite a sizable wind, *with an old ball*. And the kicking leg of the punter, Lew [sic] Gehrig, 210-pound back on Columbia's first-string eleven, was so sore from a muscular sprain as to cause a limp.

"'I never saw a better one,' was Head Coach Buck O'Neill's comment on Gehrig's punting prowess. 'Under favorable conditions, he could be doing 70 yards.'

"Eddie Mahan, the far-famed Harvard back of 1917, once stated that '37 yards is a good average for any kicker.'"

And in case you missed the point somehow despite all the language, the headline gave it to you between the eyes: "Gehrig Cheers Columbia Football Fans with Terrific Punts in Practice Games." How's that for living serenely in the eye of the hurricane?

As I said, it was a time of contrasts, sort of an age of innocence surrounded by an age of evil, rum courts surrounded by speakeasies, people going to heaven surrounded by people going to hell, and with flourishes. Gullibility on the sports pages surrounded by skepticism on the front pages. All kinds of organized fanaticism and hero-worship on the baseball or football fields—surrounded by all kinds of reality on the streets, especially where I was growing up back in Chicago. Another example of the fantasies that were surrounding the "performers" like nineteen-year-old Columbia Lou was one newspaper report just before the Dartmouth game:

"In view of the recent publicity given to the fact that Eddie Fischer wears special glasses while playing football, camera men galore journeyed up to Baker Field to get snaps of the only bespectacled footballer in action."

I always thought that was beautiful, somewhere between charming and frightening in its single-minded concentration on a guy who wore eyeglasses while playing college football and who therefore qualified as a full-time phenomenon. Lou's scrapbooks are filled with the same contrasts: runaway joy over home runs and long-yardage gains or long-yardage kicks, followed later by runaway tragedy after the cheers had faded away. Good times, bad times; happy times, sad times. Gehrig hits memorable home run over the wall at Wrigley Field (applause). Gehrig stars as running back, as tackle and as guard (applause). Gehrig makes coach feel secure before Cornell game (applause).

He could do it all, and for an encore after that grandslam home run in the intercity championship game in baseball, he would pull a few dazzlers in football. He and his old shortstop, for instance, combining for an encore: "Bunny Bunora, the Commerce High captain," reported the *Times*, "and Lou Gehrig, the 'Babe Ruth of the high schools,' contributed the plays which brought Commerce victory." That is, a football victory over Morris High by 16 to 7, like this: "Touchdowns—Bunora, Gehrig. Goal from field—Gehrig."

And then there was the day Yankee Stadium opened in the Bronx. It was April 18, 1923, and about 74,200 people crammed into the ball park, so I guess that the Yankees hadn't exactly obliged old John McGraw and gone away to "wither on the vine." Everybody was there, from

Governor Al Smith to John Philip Sousa and the Seventh Regiment Band. Oh yes, and also Babe Ruth, who obliged everybody by hitting the home run that beat the Boston Red Sox, 4 to 1.

While all that was going on in the Bronx, things were nice and quiet across the river in uptown Manhattan. I don't know if Nicholas Murray Butler, the president of Coumbia, glanced out his window that afternoon (assuming that he hadn't skipped over to watch the Yankees). But if he did glance out the window he might have spied some commotion on South Field, where his baseball team was playing Williams College—and losing, 5 to 1, even though his pitcher was a study in contrasts all by himself. Lou struck out seventeen batters, walked four and hit one, and he also was the losing pitcher. But when Columbia went to bat, he became the No. 3 hitter in the lineup, and he got two of the four hits made by Columbia against the *other* pitcher.

The headline in the *Tribune* said: "Gehrig Strikes Out Seventeen Batters, But Columbia Nine Loses to Williams by 5 to 1." Babe Ruth got some headlines that day, too, and they were a lot bigger than Lou's. But by the time the college baseball season was far along in 1923, newspaper writers were trotting out more of that deep-purple language to describe life in the well-insulated world of fun and games. One headline read: "Gehrig Biggest Star in College Baseball." And beneath it came this little digression from the world's troubles by Hugh Fullerton:

"Columbia University, emerging from the doldrums of sports and coming to the front in rowing, basketball and track, and promising to return to major rank in football, is keeping pace in baseball.

"With a new, green team, Andy Coakley, the famous old pitcher who once saved a championship for the Chicago Cubs, only to be beaten out of his honors and his money, is making trouble for the Eastern college baseball teams, and Columbia, with improved pitching, could be a candidate for the highest honors.

"Coakley has shown me the player I believe to be the coming great star of the college world, and, barring accident, a worthy successor to George Sisler. If he can hit major pitching, he may be another Babe Ruth.

"That sounds strong. Yet I have seen him hit a ball into the center-field stands—which are 418 feet from the plate, 20 feet high and 30 feet deep. He has hit the ball into the left-field seats, 400 feet from the plate, and over the right-field bleachers, which are 308 feet from the plate on the foul line.

"The boy is Lou Gehrig, football and baseball player. Gehrig has batted .540 in Columbia's games thus far this season, struck out 44 men in the four games he has pitched, and plays first base, outfield or performs on the slab."

Anyway, that was *his* world—"on the slab," at the bat, covering the bag, living up to all the clichés while his mother was keeping everybody fed and fat at the Phi Delta Theta house and his father was doing odd jobs and building the notion that maybe their son's muscles were finally pulling the family out of the strain and pinching of the last twenty years.

Back in *my* world, though, the cheering had already started to turn to tears—inside our apartment because my father had been caught on the prowl and outside our apartment because all the emotions of the postwar years seemed to be exploding in Chicago.

I can remember one incident that set the stage and the tone for the violence we all came to connect with the twenties. It began on a hot July afternoon when a black boy who had been swimming off the South Side beach crossed into the white section.

It was an unwritten law that only a small area of the beachfront was "reserved" for the growing black population of the city, and, when the black youth swam into the water of the adjoining white area, a crowd of bathers on the shore began to throw rocks at him. He crawled onto a float, where one well-aimed rock from the shore hit him on the head and knocked him back into Lake Michigan. He never surfaced, and that night all hell broke loose on the South Side.

The first reaction came when black crowds started insulting whites who were passing through. Then a couple of thousand members of Ragen's Colts, a predominantly Irish club headed by ward leaders, ward-heelers, saloon owners and small crooks, gathered in force between Forty-third and Sixty-sixth streets. They were out to teach the blacks a lesson, to keep them "in their place" was the way they'd put it. Next, a bunch of hooligans led by Ragen's Colts rampaged through the Black Belt with guns and bombs, shooting blacks on sight, dynamiting their homes and looting stores. The blacks, including many war veterans who had returned home not too long before, retaliated by burning "white" property and overturning streetcars and automobiles.

I was scared out of my wits. One reason was that my father had hidden a lot of blacks from the "lynch mobs," stashing them in the empty upper stories of his German Pavilion restaurant until the worst of the riot was over. It took four days to simmer down, at that, and by that time 34 persons had been killed and more than 500 blacks and whites alike had been seriously injured.

As bad as that was, as mad as that was, it turned out to be only the beginning of a long and continuing wave of violence that wracked Chicago while I was growing up. This one had been a racial war; what followed was more of a social war, if "social" is the word for all the corruption, graft, wheeling, dealing, muscling, bootlegging and mass killing that ruled things between the end of the war and the start of the Depression.

There was probably no way that I could have grown up untouched or unchanged by any of this. But by then it didn't take any outside pressure to chip away at the "happy hearth" that the Twitchells had been gathering around; we'd had all the pressure we could stand from my father's private life, once it had stopped being private. Things grew so shaky between him and my mother—including anonymous phone calls asking "Would you like to know where your husband is?"—that she finally took the sad step into a lawyer's office.

"Does he pay the rent?" she was asked, after she'd recited her story. "Do you have a liberal allowance? Are the children well fed and clothed?" When she answered "yes" to all the questions, wondering just what he was driving at, the lawyer got up from his swivel chair, looked her in the eye and said: "What the hell do you want to divorce a guy like that for? Besides, I think the dame herself is making all those phone calls to get you to divorce him. Forget it, and go out and enjoy yourself."

The advice might have shaken her up, but it penetrated. Almost overnight, everything started to change at our house. The bickering stopped. The "dame's" phone calls were forgotten. The big apartment began to fill up with friends, the reception room began to fill up with golf bags and even the family bootlegger began to make weekly visits. We were slipping into the throes of the Prohibition "experiment," and the master closet was getting stacked high with cases of Scotch "right off the boat." I was even teaching my kid brother how to do the Charleston.

My mother and I also started to get pretty handy with all those charge accounts that Dad had opened all over town in his own campaign to keep things moving. It wasn't exactly our entrance into the "era of wonderful nonsense," but it sort of set up the circumstances that moved us into the era, whether we liked it or not. At least, we broke out of the cocoon and headed in the general direction of the "social" whirl that was changing everybody else in town.

I think it was in the summer after the race riots when my mother and I were vacationing in South Haven across Lake Michigan—this would have been 1920—that we met Helen Brussow. She was a young married woman who became very friendly with my mother. She insisted that we look up her two sisters when we got back to Chicago in the fall.

Her sisters were married to brothers, a novel situation in itself: Dorothy was married to Harry Grabiner and Mary was married to Joe Grabiner. The girls were both beauties, too, and after we met them I was impressed and even captivated by them. About fifteen years older than I was—they were full-grown married women and I was fifteen—they still struck me as a really stylish pair of Viennese girls, Mary Pickford and Theda Bara combined. They opened the door for me to the whole range of feminine skills like fixing my hair just so and buying my clothes in the right places and, well, making my own way out of the "situation" that had forever changed things at home.

It was a strange way to win your letter. The sisters each had a car, each presented as a gift by the appropriate brother-husband. And, best of all, neither could drive, so I more or less signed on as the chauffeur for both. Shopping expeditions, rounds of golf—we did it all in Mary's yellow Electric at its full speed of fifteen miles an hour along the Chicago boulevards.

I also was impressed when I met Dorothy's husband, Harry Grabiner, and found that he was secretary and vice-president of the Chicago White Sox. Mary's husband, Joe, who was Harry's older brother, probably should have impressed me even more—he was a well-known and respected gambler, and in those days it was possible for a well-known gambler to be a respected one, too.

The story of the two brothers who married two good-looking sisters figured to be dramatic enough, but this particular story was more like a movie scenario. Joe, the older one, was a desperately poor Jewish boy from the South Side who had gone from rags to riches with four or five deluxe horse rooms and gambling parlors scattered around town. There was nothing of the mug or gangster about him, even though he must have had some associates or, shall I say, clients who might have fit that description. But I knew him till the day he died, and he was first-rate with me. He reminded me of the legendary Colonel Bradley, whom I met years later in Palm Beach, where he was more highly respected and a greater gentleman than the rich society playboys and tycoons who won and lost fortunes at his roulette wheels and crap tables.

When Joe began to make it as a gambler, he also began to put his brother Harry through college. Just like in the movies: Joe didn't want "the kid" to have to hang around the tough guys who were hanging around his business. So Harry got his education, and then his career with the White Sox, and that was the biggest tip-off to the brothers' honesty of all. The White Sox became the Black Sox in 1919 when eight of their players were indicted for having "thrown" the World Series to the Cincinnati Reds, but no hint of scandal touched either Harry in the front office of the team or his brother Joe, the gambler.

The two Grabiner women became my older sisters, in and out of our house, turning me from a sort of loner into a person with some idea what it was all about. They were a big improvement over my earlier friends, like the two girls who'd come to Chicago from a convent near Notre Dame—orphan sisters from a prominent family who'd been left a pile of money plus full control over the pile. For a while I was pretty close to *those* sisters, who may have been more sophisticated in some ways than the Grabiners. At least, they knew all the nightclubs and speakeasies, and they drank their gin in Orange Blossom and Bronx cocktails the way I drank lemonade in Jackson Park.

But that was about as far as their sophistication took me. Their boyfriends were mostly college guys, the kind we used to call lounge lizards. With their greased-down hair, hip flasks and a talent for running out of gas on midnight rides. It made my mother vaguely uncomfortable that college kids were drinking on dates, that girls wore their skirts above the knees and that they all seemed to drive around in "fast" cars. But between us, we managed to hold the line. She'd make the boys call at the house to pick me up for a date, and I'd phone her if I wanted to stay out late to catch the last show at the Frolics or dancing at the Grenada. I'd usually wind up serving the guys bacon and eggs long before my father came home at four or five in the morning. For us, Prohibition was no bargain.

I could hold my liquor, even though I was pretty far from converting to an apprentice lush. I don't remember too many days when I missed playing eighteen holes of golf or riding horseback for an hour or two, no matter how late the party had lasted the night before. After I switched my social allegiance from the poor little rich girls from the convent, I began to join Dot and Mary Grabiner in Harry's box at Comiskey Park. I got fairly sharp at the racetrack, too. When I won, I collected; when I lost, I charged it to my father's account. And between that sure-thing and a flair for poker—with the Grabiner girls and their married friends and their money—I never seemed to run short of money.

I suppose the thing that switched me off the "Irish sisters" and onto the Grabiner sisters for good was a triple date one night. Joe Grabiner had been trying to tout me off the college crowd anyway, saying they wouldn't do anything for my reputation. I got into a real flap with him for meddling, but Joe won the argument that night when my swinging young friends and their dates took us to a well-known eating place.

By then, I was well-known in speakeasy society, and I also was knowing enough to suspect that our "dates" were older than the run-of-the-mill college types and probably married, besides. I also knew that Colosimo's, though one of the best spots in town, had rooms available down the street for the free-spenders. So, as the gin flowed and my tipsy escort began to suggest that we adjourn the party "upstairs," I decided to butt out. I gave the other girls the high-sign, joined them in the ladies' room and took a fast poll. We decided to leave.

The only problem was that there were no cruising cabs in those days, especially in that neighborhood at that hour. So I put the problem to Mike "the Greek" Potzin, who had taken over as manager after Big Jim Colosimo had been gunned down in the foyer. Now, Mike the Greek had a reputation as one of the sleazier members of the whorehouse set in Chicago, and apparently he'd earned the reputation the hard way. He even was supposed to be trafficking in white slavery, netting the young girls who'd come to town to escape from the small towns in the Middle West. In other words, not a man of distinction—and there I was, throwing myself on his mercy to get me home.

I remember towering above Mike the Greek, because he was short, big reputation or not. I told him my name, with a touch of hauteur thrown in for effect. I needed a ride home, and asked him to get me one. He was great—squinting for a closer look, making the decision on the spot, clapping his pudgy hands together and summoning two giant-sized deputies from the smoke inside the main room. Maybe he was Mike the Greek, but he gave them the plot in pure Italian and they hustled me and my girl friends outside to the waiting black Cadillac.

We were probably protected by more muscle and more firepower than the Atlantic Fleet, and we were driven home in the high style of the time. That's when I finally decided that I'd be a lot better off playing poker in the long evenings with the Grabiner girls, or betting on horses in the long afternoons, or just sitting with them and watching their White Sox play the New York Yankees and Lou Gehrig.

Chicago, though, was a relentless city and the 1920s were a relentless time. A few months later, Mike the Greek was taken for a ride himself. He simply disappeared one day. He didn't rate much of a search. He didn't even rate a bronze casket like the elite of his profession. They just slid him into the Des Plaines River. When I heard about it, I sent him a mental bouquet saying, "Thanks for the ride home, Mike." Wild and woolly Chicago, indeed.

6

Chicago: The Good Old Days

Big Bill Thompson was elected mayor of Chicago in 1915 by a record plurality for a Republican. The Volstead Act, more properly known—and broken—as the National Prohibition Act, went into effect at 12:01 A.M. on January 17, 1920. And after those two momentous dates, things in my old hometown went rapidly downhill.

For one thing, Thompson proved no piker when it came to enlivening the town. He was a giant of a man, a one-time athlete and cowboy, full-time son of a real-estate tycoon, part-time Cook County commissioner and all-time performer on the political stump. He got elected promising to clean up the city, and he stayed elected making sure that nobody cleaned it up so that you could notice. He was all things to all people, and nothing in particular to anybody, except to those people behind the scenes who were setting the stage for the hell-bent years to come when I was growing up there, not quite realizing what all the commotion was about but still realizing that this was not your run-of-the-mill hometown.

I remember reading later how the city was described by a political science professor at the University of Chicago, Charles E. Merriam, who also happened to be an alderman. "Chicago is unique," he said. "It is the only completely corrupt city in America."

To keep it corrupt, especially to keep it corrupt until Prohibition arrived and guaranteed that it would stay corrupt, City Hall blinked while the "mob" put together its lineup of talent. At the head of the lineup for nearly a generation stood James "Big Jim" Colosimo, who earlier had called to New York for help from his bright nephew John Torrio, who in turn called to New York later for help from his muscular protégé Al Capone.

They formed a strange bunch who soon ran the best restaurants, served the best food, poured the best wine and rubbed elbows with the best people in Chicago. Colosimo himself was a big, fleshy man who fancied opera and who cultivated the friendship—or, at least, the patronage—of its stars, including Enrico Caruso, Amelita Galli-Curci, Mary Garden and John McCormack, and who reigned as a host at Colosimo's Café on South Wabash Avenue.

It was a spectacularly furnished place that lit up the red-hot Levee district of town with its green velvet walls and gold-and-crystal chandeliers as well as with the glitter of its clientele. Its only rival for a while—as far as sheer opulence went—may have been the Everleigh Club on South Dearborn, the fifty-room mansion run by the queenly young sisters from Kentucky, Ada and Minna Everleigh. They were not only southern beauties but also the daughters of a successful lawyer, and they parlayed their beauty and brains into a $250,000 showplace that also served the best food, wines and entertainment available and that ranked, to put it bluntly, as the fanciest whorehouse in the Middle West.

By the time Colosimo and his café reached their peak of public attention, the Everleigh girls had been shunted out of town during one of the "reform" waves that occasionally washed over the city's landscape. Then, by the time Big Bill Thompson took office in 1915, Colosimo had passed his own peak. He had met, and fallen head over heels for, a genteel young girl from Ohio who sang in a church choir by day and in Colosimo's Café by night. Finally, by the time Prohibition pried the lid off things in 1920, Big Jim had married his Dale Winter and, according to the whispers around town, had started to go "soft."

On Tuesday, May 11, 1920, he kissed Dale good-bye, headed downtown for his café in his chauffeur-driven limousine. Big Jim arrived at his place of business to receive two truckloads of bootleg whiskey and was shot dead in the vestibule with a bullet behind the right ear. His funeral three days later was the first extravaganza accorded

one of Chicago's underworld chiefs—the first of many—
and it came complete with 5,000 mourners, 53 pall-
bearers, 3 judges and 2 members of Congress.

Big Jim's sudden passing may or may not have been en-
couraged by his deputies Johnny Torrio and Al Capone,
but it thrust them onto the top rung of the lineup that he
had dominated. So for the rest of the decade, they and
their deputies ruled the scene with no interference from
City Hall and with sporadic interference from North Side
rivals like Dion O'Banion, the former altar boy and flower
fancier; South Side bootleggers like the Genna brothers,
who reportedly cleared $150,000 a month on homemade
whiskey; South Side gangs like Ragen's Colts, who had
provoked the race riot in 1919; and assorted other mobs
who soon were bullied or sweet-talked into a loose alliance—if that's the word—by Torrio, who drank nothing,
spoke softly and was devoted to his wife Anna.

The alliance, strictly a matter of convenience, had a tendency to fly apart at the seams at critical times. According
to the newspaper accounts and the lurid memoirs later,
one such time arrived after Capone and Torrio apparently
felt they had absorbed one double-cross too many from
O'Banion. The result was memorable. Three men stepped
out of a blue Jewett sedan near the Holy Name Cathedral
across the way from O'Banion's flower shop on State
Street. He was engrossed at the time in filling a mountain
of orders for expensive funeral wreaths for Mike Merlo,
the Sicilian mob overlord, who had died somewhat un-
characteristically of cancer. They entered the shop, shook

hands and then pumped six slugs at point-blank range into him.

The O'Banion funeral that followed outdid Merlo's funeral, or any other, for that matter, in the number of mourners and the gaudiness of their mourning. Twenty-six cars and trucks loaded with flowers crept into line with three bands, a police escort, about 10,000 people and—at Mount Carmel Cemetery— 5,000 more who had jammed every trolley car headed in that direction. It was sensational, and it took a phalanx of mounted cops to clear the path to the cemtery so that the mob could shed its most lavish crocodile tears for the one-time altar boy who had crossed one gang while masterminding another.

In those free-shooting days, I was growing out of my innocent teens and I happened to have a distant view from the fringe of the carnage that was ripping Chicago's streets apart. No, I wasn't a member of the cast; not even a member of the audience. Just somebody on the fringe of it all, far enough away to steer clear but close enough to the scene to feel the vibrations.

My first real look at No Man's Land was provided for the far-fetched reason that my mother's dearest friend was a rotund little Irish widow named Mrs. Tobin. She used to drop by the apartment every day for a cup of tea, but she brought with her the strange Irish penchant for wakes and funerals, and before long my mother developed the same strange hankering. It was no trick for the South Side to supply the corpses, and one of the earliest belonged to Mossy Enright, a pioneer labor racketeer and bootlegger,

who was shot dead in 1920. Mrs. Tobin was wild to go
see the funeral and, since I had just learned to drive, I was
commandeered to be the chauffeur for those two sweet
little Irish ghouls.

The Enright funeral even set the tone and the tradition
for the steady succession of gangland wakes that kept
much of Chicago's underworld wearing black during Prohibition. His widow appeared in deep mourning, shaking
hands with an endless line of characters and their flashy
molls, all murmuring things like "Sorry for your trouble"
and "He was a great guy" and other sentiments that
strayed from the mark. So did the condolences on the
white satin banners attached to the colossal floral pieces,
like "Rest in Peace, Old Pal"—from the executioner himself.

Things got so ostentatious that the funerals began to
resemble Broadway openings, or circus parades into town:
streets choked for blocks with Cadillacs, Locomobiles and
Pierce Arrows, trailed at a safe distance by the Fords (or,
in our case, the Stearns Knight) of the curious "public."
I'm not sure my mother learned to drive a car soon after
the Mossy Enright demonstration *just* to keep pace with
the times, but it's a fact that she did learn to drive then.
Pretty soon she and Mrs. Tobin were becoming regulars
on the outskirts of the funeral processions.

Once on wheels of their own, the hearse-chasers took
up their pursuit like a couple of drama critics arguing over
some innuendo in *Hamlet*. I remember once they fell into
some heated jaw-boning over the dramatic propriety of the
life-sized wax effigy of the "departed" that the mob had

propped in the back seat of an open touring car preceding the hearse, surrounded by banks of flowers. They agreed it was "colorful" and "imaginative," but disagreed on how "proper" it actually was. They later did vote unanimously, though, to condemn the use of election posters for mob politicians that were fastened to the automobiles of the chief mourners at the funeral of Hymie Weiss, who'd been gunned down in the company of two allies right in front of the cathedral. That, they felt, was going *too far*.

Part of the public clamor over all this was probably stoked by the fact that newspapers were sold by news of sports and crime, and the publishers quickly gave the public what it craved. The sports sections in Chicago were terrific, and many of our best playwrights and essayists got their training while covering baseball, football and the fights. But every paper in town also began to develop its corps of crime specialists, and pretty soon the street language of the day was enriched to include "the Tommy gun" or "the Chicago typewriter" (for the New Thompson submachine gun) and "pineapples" (for bombs or hand grenades).

My only contact with the *demimonde*, if you can call it that—outside of my brief encounter with Mike the Greek and my occasional forays with my mother, who loved chasing the funerals—was with a biggie. The Boss of Bosses, the man who had organized things between the reigns of Big Jim Colosimo and Al Capone and who continued long after to function as the elder statesman of all the gangs. That was John Torrio, whom I met through his wife, Anna.

She was a small, pleasant woman from Xenia, Ohio; she lived only four blocks from us, and for several sessions she was a member of our girls' poker group. We realized that Johnny was some kind of racketeer then, but she came across as a nice gentle person and so we accepted her as a poker partner in good standing. I guess we also were hungering for gossip, but she didn't volunteer any and the subject quickly became verboten among us, anyway.

We gathered from Anna Torrio that her husband was a quiet type, sort of a homebody. I was surprised when we started to discuss music and she told us it was his hobby. I don't think we were just looking at the underworld through rose-colored glasses; we were getting a sort of perverse thrill out of knowing and liking the wife of the man who was even the boss of the up-and-coming Al Capone.

One night, we got our big chance. The Cadillac drew up to the curb outside the apartment where we were playing, the chauffeur opened the car door and John Torrio stepped out. He rang the bell rather diffidently and Anna called him into the "playing room" and introduced him to the girls: "These are the Grabiner sisters . . . Eleanor Twitchell . . . Kitty McHie," and so on, whoever else happened to be sitting around the table.

There he was—the Godfather—small, quietly and neatly dressed, soft-spoken, the picture of respectability, looking more like the head teller of a suburban bank than the most powerful gangster in town, responsible for dozens of murders. At least, according to the press he was. We adjourned the game, considering the momentousness of the meeting, and then, believe it or not he joined us for some tea and cakes.

Torrio paid some attention that time to Kitty McHie, probably because her father was a newspaper publisher who had been running a series of articles on the criminal activity being engineered by Torrio's people—not only engineered but widened from Illinois into Indiana. Whatever the reason, Johnny Torrio was reserved and even well-spoken during that brief encounter.

When Kitty drove me home that night, I think we both got into the car a trifle dazed, murmuring "Jeez." I don't know what Torrio was murmuring to Anna as he drove her home, and I don't even know why he'd picked that night and that place for his visit. Maybe he just wanted to check out the girls and see what kind of people his wife had for poker pals. Maybe he was afraid she was going to blow the household cash. He was making millions of tax-free dollars a year, they say, but husbands are funny. Maybe he just didn't want her losing her shirt to anybody.

So you don't get the idea that we were all a bunch of birdbrains, I'd better add right away that our friendship with Anna Torrio did present a social, and an ethical, problem for our poker circle. We liked her despite her husband's activities, so we didn't ban her from the games. To her credit, though, she banned herself after the "peace treaty" imposed on the underworld by Torrio fell apart, triggering outright war among the Chicago mobs. It proved to be mayhem, too: Until Prohibition was repealed, there were more than 500 documented gang kill-

ings in Chicago, and God knows how many "disappear-
ances."

One of the few things I've learned in life is that people
are not all of a piece; they are incredibly contradictory,
and John Torrio was a prime example. In his "business,"
he was involved in every vice and crime up to and including murder. But as far as I'd ever heard, he had no—let's
say—bad habits. He didn't gamble, he didn't smoke, he
didn't drink, he didn't even like to hear profanity. And
while his boys were living it up all night with the greatest
looking dolls money could buy, he usually stayed home
playing pinochle with Anna and listening to classical
music on the phonograph.

It wasn't long after I'd met John Torrio face to face that
Anna phased herself out of our poker circle and out of our
lives. In fact, she and her husband were almost phased out
of everything. They were coming home from shopping
together one day. Anna left the limousine, her arms
loaded with parcels, and was just opening the door of their
apartment house (which didn't even have a doorman).
Johnny started to follow her out of the car when all hell
broke loose from a Cadillac across the street.

John Torrio collapsed to the ground with his jaw broken
and a bullet in his chest. His chauffeur took a bullet in the
leg. There were four men in the Cadillac forming the firing squad, and now two of them ran across the street to
finish him off. One shoved his automatic to Torrio's head,
clicked the trigger and nothing happened. He'd emptied it
unloading the first barrage.

They all took off, careening around the corner, while

Anna Torrio dragged her shot-up husband inside the lobby and called for an ambulance. It came and hurried him to the Jackson Park Hospital, where Capone posted four bodyguards in the corridor, and three weeks later they shunted him down the fire escape and home. But the message had been delivered, and Torrio took it hard: His army of 300 gunners still hadn't been able to force "peace" on the remnants of the gangs left in business after O'Banion's execution.

In any event, Torrio got the message and made the most of it. He'd been out on bail at the time for a trial in connection with a raid on one of his breweries, though with his influence and his bankroll he was considered a safe bet to beat the rap. Now, though, he apparently decided that the safest place for a while might be within the strong arm of the law—until Capone could splinter the opposition. Or maybe he wanted to protect his wife. Whatever he wanted, he suddenly pleaded guilty and took a nine-month sentence in the Lake County jail, where the warden obligingly had his cell fitted with bulletproof steel blinds, Oriental rugs, easy chairs, and a bed brought from home. Some cell; some jail.

Not only that, but special guards were assigned to patrol the corridors; not to keep Torrio in, but to keep "visitors" out. The menu was different, too: His meals were either home-cooked by his wife or delivered from Henrici's Restaurant. But within the lap of that luxury, he was a troubled man.

He knew that the O'Banion coalition wouldn't lay off until they'd finished the job, so he called in Capone and his lawyers almost every day for huddles to decide how to stay alive, if not to stay in command. He decided finally to "retire" right out of the line of fire, and he did. He turned the empire over to Capone, finished his term in prison, left in a convoy of three cars swarming with guards (his own), drove across the state line to Indiana and boarded an express for New York. He met Anna there, and they sailed for Italy, turning their backs on the jungle that Johnny Torrio had helped to create.

Putting Al Capone in charge was not the kind of move that figured to result in any "era of good feeling," not in Chicago or Cicero or anyplace else. Capone may have been Torrio's successor, but he was a completely different sort of bird as far as personal style went. Crude, gross, hungry for power, quick on the trigger, Capone would gamble on anything in sight, whether it was roulette, dice or horses, and he didn't pinch pennies when he did. Later he estimated that he'd dropped something like 10 million dollars on the horses alone during his years in Chicago.

Johnny Torrio, the man who got out of town while the getting-out was good, eventually returned to America from abroad. He even made a few visits to Chicago to preside over some crisis or other. He never stayed too long but settled instead in New York and continued to serve as chairman of the board, *ex officio*.

I saw Johnny Torrio once more, although from a distance, when my mother and I took a winter cruise from New Orleans to Havana late in the twenties and he was also on board the ship. He died in New York years later, in 1957—of natural causes.

G. K. Chesterton, the English writer, visited Chicago during those tumultuous years and concluded: "Chicago has many beauties, including the fastidiousness and good taste to assassinate nobody but assassins."

A neat turn of phrase, but not exactly accurate. Not as accurate as a conclusion reportedly made by another visitor to my town, Lucky Luciano, who was said to have been impressed by what was going on. "A real goddamn crazy place," he supposedly observed. "Nobody's safe in the streets."

7

〜

1929: No Place to Hide

I suppose that, in the 1920s, you could say I fiddled while Chicago burned. I was young and rather innocent, but I smoked, played poker, drank bathtub gin along with everybody else, collected $5 a week in allowance from my father, spent $100 a week, made up the difference from winter-book jackpots at the racetrack that filled a dresser drawer with close to $10,000 at one point, and learned to become a big tipper.

Chicago was at loose ends, too. Everybody seemed to be shooting everybody else, the cops and robbers were often on the same side, the speakeasies were doing a landslide business, young people spent a lot of time either in rumble seats or on the dance floor inventing variations on the

Charleston and generally it was no time and no place for
the faint of heart.

For shelter, I chose safely married women as golfing
partners by day and older, less eager, escorts by night.
My mother, after seeing a few Clara Bow films, finally got
the message of the times and decided to throw open our
large apartment to my friends, which was a shrewd way of
putting a roof and a lid on the festivities. And, while it
might have been jarring sometimes to our neighbors and
tenants, no one seemed to complain very much about the
noise from the piano or the constant spinning of our Vin-
cent Lopez records.

Maybe people were getting the idea that it was hazardous outdoors; especially after dark when the shooting
started between the "soldiers" of the gangs who were
marauding through town. Maybe you didn't actually hear
the shots, but you always could read about them in the
headlines the next day.

Sometimes the pressure was relieved by little ironic
touches, like geography. If a hood was picked off one
night on the South Side, you could bet that the next bit of
gunplay would take place on the North Side. So the "all-
clear" could be sounded at least until the score was evened
up. Besides, their marksmanship was considered phenomenal: I don't recall many "innocent bystanders" who were
knocked off during the street skirmishes. I don't recall *any*,
actually; but I wouldn't want to stake the history of those
days on the memory of a teen-ager who was growing up
thinking about the more normal things in life; like the
turkey trot.

Along the way, some of the girls and I started our quiet little hen game of poker once a week. We'd hold it at somebody else's house each time, toss in a buffet lunch, and make it an afternoon.

Looking back on it, though, I'd have to say that I was a good kid. And the Grabiner sisters made sure that I stayed that way. The big goal for me was a rich husband—at least, that was everybody else's big goal for me—and that was the thing in those days: Everybody had to marry a millionaire.

However, the sisters were so strict with me that once I referred to my mother as "my old lady" and they stepped all over me. It didn't have anything to do with honor among thieves; it was just that they were fairly strait-laced people in the middle of the savages who were shooting and looting the town.

Take our poker game, for instance. It included Anna Torrio, whose husband outranked the mayor and governor and maybe even the president of the United States in raw power; Mary Grabiner, whose husband Joe outranked most of the "independent" gamblers in town; her sister, Dot Grabiner; Kitty McHie, whose father owned the *Hammond Times* and who was always crusading against the gangster element; and myself—Eleanor Twitchell, the teen-aged daughter of the chief concessionaire for Chicago's park system.

No booze flowed at our poker marathons, and I was just about the only one who smoked. But it developed into a lively little game where the stakes inched upwards and somebody might run out of cash and then suggest: "I'll give you a hundred for that dress you bought yesterday."

My own merry-go-round started to slow down one day when I felt dizzy on the golf course and decided to visit the family doctor. He was a kindly old man with a beautiful head of silvery white hair and a pointed goatee to match, something like a Norman Rockwell painting of a family doctor as he might have appeared in the twenties.

I told him what had happened. He listened to my heart and then he gently informed me that I had a heart leakage. No treatment, I just had to slow down and quit racing through the day playing golf, riding horses and kicking my way into the Charleston. All of a sudden, I had to die a little in order to live a little.

I remember driving home and realizing that I also must now be rated a menace behind the wheel. The doctor hadn't gone so far as to tell me that, but the shock of what he did say left me convinced that I was coming apart at the seams. When I got home, I broke down in my mother's arms like a little girl—and now she had an "invalid" daughter on her hands along with a young son to raise and a husband who drank and cheated and ran her a merry chase.

Maybe Chicago's wild pace didn't slow down after that, but mine did. Books took the place of my daily golf round, philosophy crept in and replaced the long, late hours I'd been keeping in noisy restaurants and cabarets. I don't think I ever turned into an intellectual, but I did begin to read people like Voltaire, Thoreau and even Spinoza. I became taken with the new approaches to psychology of Freud, Jung and Adler. And I switched from being a

sports-oriented member of Chicago's semijet set (without
the jets) into a book-oriented invalid spinster vaguely in
the self-styled mold of Elizabeth Barrett Browning. On
the plus side, I managed to get myself relieved of all
household duties, now that I was considered a delicate
person.

That final little role of mine may have been the last
straw, though, because Mary Grabiner decided she
couldn't take it any longer and whisked me off to her doctor, a highly publicized man who already was becoming
something of a celebrity because he was blind and therefore was supposed to be a wizard in diagnosing the beats
or missed beats of the heart. We seemed to make everything into a soap opera in those days.

The celebrity doctor lived up to his notices, all right.
Flanked by several assistants, who probably added to his
prestige and his fee, he checked my heart solemnly before
and after I did some exercises, like jumping up and down
a dozen or so times. The more I jumped and the more he
checked, the more I worried that he'd confirm the earlier
diagnosis and even go far beyond it.

But when we were finished, he told me that my condition wasn't so serious after all. I'd have to avoid high alti-
tudes, bicycle riding and debilitating love affairs. That's
right, debilitating love affairs. But those three things
meant no great sacrifice for me, because I had no known
reason to visit Denver, I loathed bicycle riding and, if he
meant what I thought he meant on Point Number 3, I had
never been debilitated.

My heart was "compensating," he said, and that relieved me somewhat—whatever that meant. But I still came away with a heart neurosis that was to linger for years and that would change my life. It wasn't just that I began cutting down golf rounds from eighteen holes to nine. But it got me involved even deeper into the new "loves" that had appeared during my sedentary period before the checkup. Things like books and literature, which I'd always been able to take or leave in my class-cutting days. I remember the first time I cried over Anna Karenina and her tragic love life, my resentment at the Dreiser character who dumped his pregnant girl friend in the lake in *An American Tragedy*, and my sympathy for the girls in the scandalous but beautifully written book *The Well of Loneliness*. Doctors didn't test hearts with electrocardiograms in those days, and it took many years before I discovered that my heart really wasn't "bad." But we thought so then and, after growing up as a distinguished school dropout, I suddenly became a drop-in—under false premises.

I even used to sneak into Thornton Wilder's classes at the University of Chicago, though I'd never bothered to go to college before. I didn't actually go to college this time, either. I'd just wander into his classes and try to get lost in the crowd. I always felt that he knew I wasn't officially in the class, but he would still correct the papers I'd turn in, answer my questions about his lectures and patiently discuss literature with me afterward.

Another change in my outlook involved—well, men. It hadn't seemed important until I reached my twenties, but now I began to think seriously about marriage. My life had been full enough, but I started to feel that as much fun as I was having, even with a weak heart, it just wasn't enough to build a life on.

The trouble probably wasn't with me, anyway; more likely it was with my boyfriends. Some were good-looking, some had charm, but none had that certain something I'd been looking for. Maybe those things were okay for a date, but not for getting married. After you got married, you couldn't come up with the excuse that you couldn't see your husband tonight because you had another date. My own father had looks and charm, and I remembered what happened to him. So I wanted to be very sure.

For a while, I became interested in one delightful young man who looked as though he might be the answer (now that I'm sifting *all* the little surface memories from the "change" in my outlook on life). But that one blew up in the kitchen. I was trying to find the right pan or some such thing to prepare a midnight snack, and he just sort of got fed up while I shopped around. Fed up, but not fed. He muttered something like "Why don't you learn your way around the kitchen?" It was his first and last crack.

Another suitor came from a wealthy family who was visiting Chicago from New Orleans. He gave me a terrific rush, but that time I was the first one who cooled off. I found out that, at the age of twenty-five, he'd already been to the altar twice. Then I cooled off all the way when he introduced me to his traveling psychiatrist.

The big block, though, probably was the fact that I just couldn't change my attitudes or style of living overnight. I certainly couldn't change my family's troubles overnight.

The main thing there was that my father kept getting more and more involved with his golfing pals and his girl pals. He'd even go off to Florida alone each winter for a golfing vacation, while my mother and I were "paid off" with a trip to the Kentucky Derby each spring plus a stay at French Lick, the fashionable spa near Louisville, before returning to our year-round troubles in Chicago.

I spent one summer working for my father and was appalled to see that his chief deputy would show up for work drunk. Besides, Dad's girl friend was working as a cashier and apparently was dipping into the till to her heart's content. His intricate system for running the park concessions started to break down because no one else was minding the store. And finally, like most of the people we knew, he invested in some crocodile acreage during the Florida land boom of the twenties, and he literally sank his cash into the swamp.

When Prohibition started in 1920, I remember that he put away two cases of Scotch; prudently put them away, I suppose you'd say. At his rate of consumption then, they figured to last the duration. But toward the end of the decade, he and his friends were swallowing that much Scotch every couple of weeks.

So things were getting sticky enough, between my father's business life and his mixed-up domestic life. But they were bound to get even stickier because his lease as the parks concessionaire was running out, too, and it was no secret that he was losing his grip on that, as well.

The time came for new bids to be filed by people trying to win the lease on the park concession business. You'd

think that my father would have the inside track, since
he'd been operating the business all those years, but he
was practically living out of the bottle by then and was in
no shape to regroup his forces or his money. I remember
the crowning touch, one night when I was in the Bal
Tabarin room of the Sherman House hotel. It was a fancy
place where you'd have to make reservations ahead of time
and dress for dinner.

A real-estate man, sort of semilegitimate with City Hall
connections, came over to my table and whispered to me:
"You're Eleanor Twitchell, aren't you? Tell your old man
he better bid a hundred and ten thousand or he'll lose
his lease."

Next morning, I told my father what had happened and
he hit the ceiling. Just stiffened and sort of snarled to me:
"You and your goddamn gangster informers can go to
hell." Just like that.

Anyway, he went ahead and submitted a bid based on
his own calculations. And sure enough, he didn't bid
enough. It was decided that the concession lease had been
awarded to an unknown partnership—previously unknown, at any rate—and my father was temporarily "retired." He took it with his old doomsday guts, too. Pre-
tended it didn't make a shred of difference, headed for a
golfing spree in Biloxi, Mississippi, on the Gulf Coast and
then sauntered over to visit Uncle Gene and the ponies in
New Orleans.

When my father finally got back from his holiday, I
began to get an empty feeling in my head and in my
pocketbook, especially when he began to poor-mouth

around the house. Now that he was retired and all that, we'd all have to cut down on our spending. He even set the example for us by switching from Scotch to bathtub gin. The Twitchells were still ahead of the times: We were going broke *before* the Depression.

Somewhere along the line, I went to business school on a kind of premonition. I'd get the same premonition whenever my father wanted to pull a real-estate deal, like putting up a building, but would usually complain, "God, but money's getting tight." Anyway, now that it was really getting tight, I enrolled at the Gregg Business School for a six-month course. I guess I was running out of choices, but I knew one thing—I also was running out of that $10,000 that I'd won at the track years before.

If you need to be reminded how families get wind of a depression around the corner, and how the depression finally flattens families after it turns the corner, this was how it worked on us. My father had stock in a chain of banks called the Bain Banks, and the bank hit the skids just when his new building project was nearly finished; all but the roof. He had enough money left to complete the building, an apartment building that was supposed to form our next nest egg, and he did complete it. Then the Depression leveled everybody in town and he found that he couldn't rent out the apartments in his brand new building. Nobody had the $200 a month for the rent.

Meanwhile, I was plugging along at Gregg learning shorthand and other things that seemed a far cry from the old poker games. But before I got through the course there, one of my friends got the job of hiring the staff for the swanky new store that Saks Fifth Avenue was putting up on North Michigan Avenue near the Drake Hotel. I didn't know what job to apply for because I'd never worked in my life and I'd only finished four months of the six-month course at Gregg. But it was easy for a young girl to become a secretary at the end of the "Roaring Twenties," especially if she looked trim, prim and efficient in a freshly starched white collar and business-like black dress. So when my friend said, "Get over here, we're hiring help like crazy," I put on my best Kay Francis costume and somehow got myself hired.

To oblige them, I said I was a file clerk, even though they had no files in the place and I wasn't a clerk; only piles of rubble around and all kinds of crates. We were sitting on crates going through the motions when the elegant new manager arrived from New York. He asked me if I could type and handle correspondence and, when I made with a little white lie, I was promoted to secretary to the general manager of the swankiest store in town.

The store opened in March, 1929, and was an immediate success, and everyone was happy and busy—until October. Then in a series of bombshell sessions, the stock market crashed and the wildest spree in American history was over. All of a sudden, we were left with the long and miserable hangover of the Depression. Soup kitchens, long lines of wondering, wandering people; no such things as unemployment insurance or Social Security; no money, no job and, worse, no hope. Some of my father's well-to-do friends, his golfing pals and Florida cronies who had thought nothing of betting hundreds on a horse race or buying their girl friends mink coats, began to follow the compulsion that was sweeping financial circles: to jump from high buildings or stick their heads into the oven before the gas company disconnected service for non-payment.

It was no bargain, but we were comparatively lucky in my family. I had a job that paid $30 a week, and I treasured it so much that I'd even get up at five o'clock in the morning, take the Sixty-seventh Street trolley to the Illinois Central train that took me in turn to Randolph Street, then the bus to Saks on the near North Side. At night, I'd reverse my steps, and long ones they were. I did it because people were panting for jobs as saleswomen, even though there suddenly were no customers in the store for the saleswomen to sell to. Things got so tight that I even tried to help some friends who'd been living high until then. By that time I'd been nudged up to a sort of "director of personnel." Even some baronesses I knew came around, looking for a job.

It was a wild change in a department store, as though a bomb had gone through the place. And it was a wild change in me. It was just a terrible blow, a real haymaker, the family getting cuffed around, but no favors were asked and none given. The poker game with the girls was forgotten. I didn't cry on anybody's shoulder, though. I just took it and grew up fast. Thousands of others did, too. A lot of them even grew *old* fast.

My kid brother, who had been promised an appointment to West Point by a congressman, left school and also got a job. And we moved into Dad's building—his almost-unfinished symphony—while the rents came tumbling down from $200 a month to $85, and that was for six rooms, two baths and a lovely glass sunparlor. They were superluxury apartments; a beautiful building, and it became an albatross around his neck.

This is the way it would drag him downhill: He already had a big first mortgage on the building, he couldn't rent out the apartments in it, he cut the rent in stages, the few tenants began to double up to accommodate their jobless relatives. Dad took a second mortgage, and he kept the whole creaky thing afloat a little longer.

He also kept drinking a little longer and, when he finally couldn't take things the way they were turning out, he simply left. Went back down to New Orleans, where he'd worked with Uncle Gene, the track price maker, and got back to working again for him at the Fairgrounds, which was a gorgeous track then. As a farewell flourish, and probably a smart one, he put the sinking apartment building in my name because he'd been threatened with some lawsuits.

As a matter of fact, he did go through one suit and I got involved in that one, too, even though it turned out to be a kangaroo court. One magistrate sat at a table hearing all the small claims, then my father came in and said he didn't have any money (and he may have been telling the truth). I sat there waiting for our turn at bat, and I knew most of the facts pretty well—every month I had to go down to the bank to deposit money for the janitor and the other services we were supposed to be providing in the building. The bank sort of hoped we'd keep putting some money in, because it certainly didn't want to take over another losing proposition like a half-vacant apartment building, anyway.

Don't ask me how, but we won that case in spite of the long legal odds. We didn't win much else, though; in fact, we lost our collective shirt. And after my father took off for New Orleans, my mother used to look in wonder at her two new "providers," since my brother and I would plunk our salaries into her lap every payday.

But things weren't so hot at Saks, either. The store still stands in my memory as one of the real towering symbols of the Depression: It was one place in town where everybody else's business came across your desk in big, black, overdue-account numbers.

The store had opened with all kinds of flourishes, and all kinds of salespeople had quit the established stores like Marshall Field and Carson, Pirie, Scott to join the glamorous new place with the floorwalkers in striped pants and white carnations in their lapels. The floorwalkers even came equipped with fancy titles like "department head." But then, almost everybody came equipped with titles; mine had been secretary to the general manager and director of personnel.

The sad part of it, though, slipped across my desk every day in the credit statements. They amazed me because some of our highest-standing citizens in town had some of our lowest-standing credit ratings. It was probably the fault of the guy's wife in a lot of cases; she would get caught up or carried away with things, and later file the monthly bill in the incinerator until somebody at the store started to do a little howling. I suppose that I was the "somebody" who did the howling a lot of the time. I even started a file with a neat little credit code mark at the top of each card; things like S.P. (slow pay) or A (reasonably fast), maybe AA (unusually fast); maybe a big fat old D (owes everybody in town).

After the market crashed that October, we got around to admitting that we were overstaffed. So then we started to do our firing on Friday afternoons. That's where my *other* title came in: director of personnel. At first, it meant I did the hiring; later, the firing. And after a while, when one of the girls was told to "see Miss Twitchell" on a Friday afternoon, she'd just get up and pick up her things and go home. After a time, they began to hate me the way I began to hate both my titles.

I guess if you live by the sword, you die by the sword. After living through three managers at Saks, I saw Number 4 arrive and before long I saw him fire *me*. Miss Twitchell had been sacked by Saks.

I lived a lot during the Prohibition years in my "wild and woolly town," and I learned a lot about living during the Depression years—like how to be a wife. That was one thing I'd never come close to being, and although I didn't suspect it then, I was getting awfully close. Out there somewhere was Lou Gehrig, who'd been visiting Chicago three times every summer on business—the business of baseball—while everybody else's business was sinking out of sight.

If I hadn't gone through the Depression the way I did, I probably would've married a rich man, since people were always trying to match me with one. But I did go through it and I did get cuffed around. And after our paths finally did cross, we wouldn't have made it if it hadn't been *for* the Depression—and Gregg shorthand. Somehow, they converted me from the heady world of unreality in the twenties into the desperate world of reality starting in the thirties. And though I couldn't have guessed it then, a great deal of reality was gathering around me.

8

Gehrig, 1b

IT took guts to build a World's Fair and to call it the Century of Progress in the middle of the Depression. It was like rounding up the bread line from downtown Chicago, loading the people onto a bus, carting them over to the lakefront near Soldiers Field and telling them to forget their miseries and the jobs that didn't exist, and then regaling them for days on end with brilliant spiels about all the progress flowing their way from this great century of ours.

It also took guts for me to leave my cushy job at Saks after I'd been dumped, get into my car and start driving home to join the army of people looking for jobs. I was crying slightly as I left the store for the last time that day in 1931, but I guess that the realities of life had toughened me up during my days as a "working girl." I stopped the car as I was passing the place where they were building the Century of Progress and then for no good reason I pulled over and parked. This was no flashy sports runabout, not the sort I'd more likely been driving during the salad days of Prohibition. Just a secondhand car bought for transportation. I got out and walked straight into the Administration Building and into a new beehive of activity. Before I left the building, I'd been sort of adopted by that merry crew of people who were constructing the modern buildings with the fairly rakish lighting and all kinds of gimmicks that were supposed to represent the great and glorious future. Not only adopted but hired as a secretary at $40 a week—with a bonus of World's Fair bonds that would be paid when I eventually quit. I had been out of work for about half an hour.

They were a strangely spirited bunch, and everybody seemed hell-bent on making the fair a showcase for the "progress" that was either behind us or ahead of us. It sure wasn't *with* us right then and there. They were headed by Rufus Dawes, the brother of Vice-President Charles Dawes, the man who had lectured Congress somewhat innocently on "the reign of terror and lawlessness" sweeping over Chicago and every place else in the 1920s. They had big architectural firms like Skidmore & Owings, all kinds of engineering experts crawling around the site and more slide rules and crystal balls to measure the "future" than you could imagine.

A combination of ideas and values were working for

them, and the result could be called something like "gaudy good taste." There were to be no Little Egypts to hoot-chie-kootchie around the midway and steal the thunder from the local talent, and the concessions were to be strictly guarded against the boys from the mob—who had already been "casing the joint" to see how they might land a piece of the action with all that money swirling around Lake Michigan.

The people running the fair were trying to put the accent on the scientific and social marvels of the time, things like the Hall of Science, the main event of the Fair, where scientists from all over the world could exhibit or study the experimental gadgets on display. My boss was the chief engineer, J. C. McConnell, whose job was to make sure that the gadgets all worked. Somebody would press a button and, presto! lights would come on flooding the whole area with sparklers and rays and special effects. No spotlights, just gentle, maybe sensual colored bulbs blending together; "indirect lighting" they were calling it. All the big companies were in on it, and I guess the idea was to take everybody's mind off the rotten today and project it into the stunning tomorrow.

We secretaries and the others on the staff all had our offices in the Administration Building, where the business and science experts from overseas and from around the country would drop by. They were looking for space to display their products, and we'd spend hours riding them around the grounds to show off the empty spaces that were still available.

I remember one smiling Japanese architect who had a

small truckload of blueprints and a whole stack of tiny
building blocks. It was a miniature building, and he
showed us how it would be put together stick by stick,
with the larger pieces of flat lumber fitting into the pieces
of upright lumber until a whole small building stood there
with absolute precision but without a single nail or splash
of cement. An indestructible jigsaw puzzle with a purpose:
to keep standing regardless of wind, snow, sleet or anything whipping in off the lake. No steel girders; just a tiny
and affable little Japanese architect who knew something
about putting up a building that might last out an earthquake.

There was no graft around the place, but not because
some people didn't try. Once someone even tried to
wheedle me. A friend of a friend of mine wanted to meet
me on business. We met for lunch and the pitch came
quickly. Some of the "boys" had a lot of cash to work
with, and they wanted to build a "dignified" thing, something like a chapel in the Fair. They supposedly had the
mummified body of John Wilkes Booth, and they had
been exhibiting it at fairs around the country, where
they'd assembled that pile of cash.

At the fairs, they would place old "John Wilkes Booth"
on view, then sell booklets on the "true and heretofore-un-
told story" of Lincoln's assassination. If that wasn't
enough to catch my attention, they even hinted that they'd
cut me in on the profits if they got the green light to
operate.

I hustled back to the office, flounced in to the boss and
announced that I was quitting for a better job. "Doing

what?" he asked, giving me all the room I needed for whatever mischief I was up to. "Vice-president of a corpse," I said.

After we had stopped laughing, he shook his head and got more serious.

"You know," he said, "that little punk is only the beginning. The pressure will come from higher and higher, and the first mistake we make, we'll find the old Everleigh Club operating full swing right next door to the Hall of Science on opening day."

Well, we didn't. But before you think I'm claiming that we were either the smartest or the most civic-minded types in town, I'll tell you what we *did* find in the center of things on opening day: Sally Rand. She became the principal dash of spice that they permitted on the premises, fan dance and all. That was no gimmick, just great business. Whenever the Century of Progress threatened to run short of cash, there was always little Sally and her dance routines, packing in the crowds and helping to pay the bills for science and technology.

At important times, like Election Night in 1932, we'd push our way into the Radio Room and listen to the returns. We all had the notion that somehow Franklin Roosevelt was going to end the Depression. Sort of a saviour. A victim of polio, he often needed to be carried around from chair to desk. Handicapped, maybe to some people; though I don't remember that we dwelled on that very much. Instead, we saw those broad shoulders and noble head and heard that sonorous voice telling us there was nothing to fear "but fear itself." Even if we hadn't been so fond of Rufus Dawes and considered him our direct link to the White House, we would have responded emotionally to Roosevelt. And so would you, if you had lived through the shattering years of the Depression.

One day after a long session of Progress at the fairgrounds, I was getting off the trolley car at my corner when I spotted my old friend and poker-playing neighbor, Kitty McHie. She was backing through the door of her apartment building with her arms full of beer bottles. We traded hellos and a few pieces of chitchat, and then she said: "Lou's coming over. Drop up for a buffet later."

"Lou's coming over" . . . just like that. Lou Gehrig, the baseball player. I'd caught a glimpse of him a few times when the Chicago White Sox were playing the New York Yankees, and once I'd even met him for a few minutes with Babe Ruth. They were great pals, then, and much in demand socially. While I was playing little games growing up in Chicago, Lou had been playing football and baseball games growing up in New York. And now he was "coming over" to Kitty's house.

Handsome, I thought. Big, handsome, successful. And painfully shy. . . .

In April, 1923, when Al Capone was terrorizing Chicago and Babe Ruth was terrorizing the American League, I was an eighteen-year-old devotee of the good life and Lou Gehrig was a twenty-year-old devotee of the hard life. His mother and father were still working at the Phi

Delta Theta house at Columbia, where Lou spent his springtime afternoons pitching and hitting baseballs for Andy Coakley's varsity.

Yankee Stadium, the newest showpiece in the big leagues, had opened for business that month. But one of the people who often skipped the wonders of the stadium was a onetime catcher named Paul Krichell, now a full-time scout for the Yankees with a special eye for college undergraduates. He followed the Columbia team to New Brunswick, New Jersey, one day, saw Gehrig play right field amusingly, then saw him whack two home runs into the trees ringing the Rutgers ball field, and Krichell didn't find that too amusing.

A couple of afternoons later, Krichell watched Coakley's team play Penn on South Field, just off Broadway at 116th Street in upper Manhattan. Gehrig pitched that time against Walter Huntzinger of Penn, the best college pitcher in the East that year. It was 2 to 2 in the ninth inning when Gehrig finally untied it—with his bat. They say it was a king-sized shot off one of Huntzinger's fastballs, and it carried across 116th Street and bounced on the steps of the library.

It was a fairly far-fetched thing, they tell me. Afterwards, Krichell pushed his way into the Columbia dressing room, held out his hand and said through the crowd: "I'm Paul Krichell. I scout for the Yankees."

Next came the question: "Have you signed with any major league ball club yet?"

Answer: "Why, no," as though it had never occurred to anybody.

Question: "Anybody else talk to you?"

Answer, sort of not convinced: "No, I never thought—"

"Well, I'm talking to you," Krichell went on. "I'm talking business to you right now. Would you like to play with the Yankees?"

Answer, painfully shy, all right: "Are you serious?"

He was serious, and the next morning Krichell and Ed Barrow signed Lou to a contract. They gave him $1,000 as a bonus, which went straight to pay hospital bills for his mother. The Yankees actually shelled out $1,500, but $500 was subtracted by a "friend" who had acted as an intermediary for Lou, sort of a finder's fee. The only thing wrong with that was that Lou hadn't known about the subtraction. When he did find out, he never spoke to his "friend" again. His mother was certain that he'd ruined his life by giving up the engineering career that she had scrimped and saved and schemed for. So she gave Lou hell for signing, and, for good measure, she also gave hell to his father.

So Lou was going to be a professional ballplayer instead of a distinguished engineer, in spite of all his mother's gripes and groans. And when school ended that June, he reported to the Yankees and their musclemen—Babe Ruth, Bob Meusel and all the others in their gleaming new stadium across the river in the Bronx. Lou stayed there just long enough to shake hands, then was handed a railroad ticket to Hartford in the Eastern League for what they used to call "seasoning," and somehow that seemed to satisfy his mother a little. Maybe "pacify" would be a better word. She thought it sounded like "Harvard," which

may have made up for the fact that Lou had forsaken
Columbia and all that it promised.

A little while later, she began to receive Lou's paychecks in the mail, and they pacified her even more. In
fact, from the time Lou got his first Yankee paycheck until
she died, Mom Gehrig never worked another day in her
life. Nor for that matter did Pop Gehrig. The pacification
of Mom Gehrig was complete.

There was one funny little wrinkle when Lou turned
pro in that spring of 1923. The first time he met Miller
Huggins, the harassed little manager of the Yankees,
Huggins asked Lou sort of hopefully if he was Jewish. He
asked it hopefully because the Yankees, even in those
days, were looking for a Jewish star—one who would have
been a "natural" in a city with so many Jewish sports fans.
Lou probably disappointed Huggins by saying no, but
Huggins overcame his disappointment and even kept Lou
around for part of that season and the next one: thirteen
games in 1923 and ten in 1924, between his "seasoning"
spells in Hartford.

Actually, there was just no vacancy for Lou on the
team—not that team. The Yankees had never won anything from the time they started doing business as the
Highlanders in 1903 until they won their first American
League pennant in 1921, the year after Ruth had arrived

I'd met him for the first time in the White Sox ball park when the
lordly Yankees visited Chicago. I don't remember who proposed to
whom. We just plotted and planned, and so, as they say, we were married. It was 1933. (Associated Press Photo)

My man—"my Luke" is what I called him—and I settled into the apartment in New Rochelle. They were the happiest days of my life, and that was one of the known facts. The unknown fact was that they would last just six years.

I was no "society girl," whatever the newspapers said in their flights of fancy; but I had grown up with more involvement in "society" than Lou, just as he had grown up with more involvement in the world of professional sports. . . .

. . . whatever I was, I looked like this only after some makeup artist in Hollywood had supplied me with the "movies" look of the 1930's from the bag of magic.

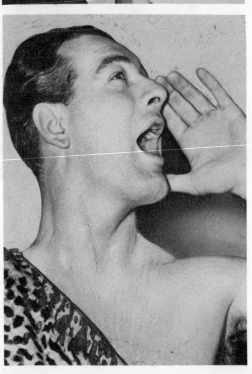

from Boston. Then they won ninety-eight games, lost fifty-five, played before more than 1,200,000 fans and began to crowd McGraw's Giants as the big club in town. In 1922, the Yankees won again, though McGraw managed to hold back the tide again in the World Series between the two New York teams. But in 1923, the tide turned. The Yankees made it three pennants in a row, knocked the Giants off their peak in the Series and became the dominant power in baseball for the next forty years.

Teams like that didn't particularly hang out "welcome" signs for college dropouts, especially when they had somebody like Wally Pipp already established at first base, and Pipp was a professional hitter and a smooth fielder. Gehrig could hit all right, but he was clumsy around first base, so he didn't get to do much for the Yankees except pinch hit and play an occasional turn at first base. Still, Lou hit .423 in limited appearances the first summer and .500 (six hits in twelve times at bat) the second summer, and he even hit his first big-league home run. But he saw more of Hartford than New York until 1925, when he hit twenty home runs for the "big team," and got out of Hartford for good.

In those days, the minor leagues were better and more important in baseball than they are now, but they were still a long way from Broadway. The Yankees traveled in a private railroad car, the farmhands went by coach. The

He was beautiful: 6 feet tall, 205 pounds strong, sturdy as a rock and innocent as a waif—no matter what Hollywood did to *him*, either.

Yankees stayed in first-class hotels and played in big stadiums before big crowds, the farmhands lived in hovels
and went to work in small parks before small audiences.
Besides, the farmhands were a combination of fading veterans who were a little bitter about life and pushy kids
clawing at a chance to escape. The former did a lot of
drinking, the latter did a lot of maneuvering and backbit-
ing. In the middle was Gehrig; homesick, straight, ob-
viously being groomed for the high life.

For a while, he reacted to his "exile" from home by div-
ing into a slump on the field. But after flirting with the notion that maybe this wasn't for him, he suddenly began to
pull clear of it and became a very big man in Hartford,
Connecticut. Working with a coach named Pat O'Connor,
Lou hit seven home runs in seven days and eighteen home
runs in forty-eight games. In the clippings in my scrapbook, it came out this way in one headline: "Lefty Lou
Gehrig at Present Ratio Would Hit 57 Homers in Full
Season." It was a mouthful, all right. Below that, the old
comparison: "Former 'College Babe Ruth,' Now a Hartford Leaguer, Has Crashed Out 18 in 48 Games."

Not bad, and he was still muscle bound from all those
body-building exercises he did at the *Turnverein* where his
father used to hang out.

Even with all those press clippings, though, Lou had almost no chance of breaking into the Yankee lineup with all
its veteran stars. But Huggins was finally forced to keep
him in New York after the 1924 season because five of the
seven other teams in the league refused to "waive" Lou out
of the league back to Hartford for still more of the "sea-

soning." The problem was that the Yankees couldn't send him "down" to the minor leagues again unless they first offered him for sale to the other clubs. Once five of the other teams expressed fast interest in him, Huggins was obliged to reel Lou in and keep him around the stadium.

So there he was, playing occasionally at first base or in the outfield whenever no great risks were involved, and trying to live up to the image of his new nickname: Buster. I suppose that meant he could bust the ball with his bat. Also that he was still a kid among older men. Whatever it meant, he stayed and gradually developed a "father fixation" for the scrawny little manager who evidently found Lou's modesty and shyness a refreshing change from the carousing bravado of the rest of the roster.

You have to picture Lou Gehrig as an awkward twenty year old the day he joined the "big club." He was big, he had big ability, he had big promise. What he didn't have was big money. Lou had reported to the training camp at New Orleans with a cardboard suitcase and $14 in his pocket. The players' expenses were paid by the club, but their salaries didn't start until the opening of the regular season. So Lou even resorted to tricks like walking from the team's hotel to the ball park, just to save cab fare. No Maseratis or Porsches in those days, no business managers or agents or huge bonus checks. Just a chance to earn a job, maybe, and the chance to earn the first paycheck six weeks later.

When Lou reported, in his later seasons, to the Yankees' new training camp in St. Petersburg, Florida, he was still lugging the cardboard suitcase. But not for long. Once he made the club, his finances started a steady climb upward into the neighborhood—financially speaking—that none of the Gehrigs had ever encountered. With his first decent salary, he did the all-American thing: He bought his mother a beautiful white house on a corner in New Rochelle in Westchester County, New York, north of the crowded Yorkville neighborhood where they had struggled for so long.

It was a revolution for a family that for such a long time had lived on the short end of life. A revolution in personal relationships, too. For one thing, Lou now became head of the new house—after all, he not only had paid for it but had gained a suddenly imposing status outside its walls as well as inside. He was still shy and quiet, even insecure; he still deferred to his mother's wishes. But Pop Gehrig's word no longer was law. If there was an inner mechanism to that, it probably involved Mom Gehrig: She now was a person of some standing and position, she finally had won her long battle of penny-pinching to make her son a success. It was as simple as that.

She now not only stood up to Pop, she began to overrule him. And Lou was relieved that he finally could repay her for the years of menial work and sacrificing. It may have been a little hard on Pop Gehrig, but perhaps there's no such thing as poetic justice in life. So he adjusted to the new order by becoming a baseball "expert," a minor celebrity as the father of Lou Gehrig. But never inside the house in New Rochelle.

The other Yankees regarded Lou as something of a young tightwad because he was still the austere Boy Scout type who didn't do much drinking except for a beer or two and who didn't suffer many temptations from the high life. He simply had never acquired the habit of spending money, even after he began to earn it.

It was no easy job for his mother to step up in class, either. Her new neighbors in the suburbs seemed standoffish, and she still had that thick German accent standing between her and an easy conversation over the backyard fence. She was even suspicious of the local merchants, especially now that the family had some money and reputation and now that Lou spent a lot of each summer traveling with the team. She went so far as to buy a kitchen scale for checking up on the town butcher's weights. No sir, nobody was going to "take" her now. And for good measure, she'd sometimes sneak away to visit her old cronies back on Amsterdam Avenue or in Yorkville, where life had been manageable even when it had been meager.

Her sense of loneliness faded, though, when Lou started bringing his new chums home, and one of her great favorites became the rough-and-ready (and hungry) Babe Ruth. Ballplayers usually are enormous eaters and, even though Mom Gehrig was still tight with a dollar, she put out many memorable meals that the hungry Yankees snapped up. She became the "hostess" of the house instead of just the servant; she also became the "star" of some of the sportswriters' columns about the newest Yankee. Then, if she needed any more ego-building, it was supplied by Ruth's mighty appetite over her mighty meals—thick vegetable soup, whole suckling pig with apple-in-mouth, potatoes or potato pancakes, double slices of pie and slabs of ultraheavy cheesecake. To say nothing of the *spécialité de la maison:* pickled eels, which Ruth would wolf down between innings of games, especially when he happened to be in a hitting slump and needed some supernourishment.

It got to be ridiculous. Every year, some sportswriter would pick up the bit about the pickled eels and then would find some connection between them and Lou's improving performances, as well as Ruth's home-run production. It got to be a legend that Lou had been practically weaned on pickled eels, which was the reason he became such a physical brute. Nonsense like that. I even read about the eels in Chicago before I knew him. After we were married, I'd tease Lou by asking him if he missed his favorite delicacy. And he'd reply by warning me to keep the damned things off our table.

When the Yankees were on a home stand, the house filled up with ballplayers and writers, and Mrs. Gehrig reached her full glory. There was a parrot on the front porch, canaries inside, a big noisy dog running around the house, home-brewed elderberry wine in the kitchen and a chihuahua named "Judge" who would slide off her large lap. Nobody knew where he got a straight name like "Judge" until people realized she'd named it for the hero of the cast, George Herman Ruth. And she called *him* "Judge," too.

While all this was going on, Lou's real career with Huggins' team began quietly on June 2, 1925, when he went in to play first base for Wally Pipp—and stayed there for fourteen years. They said that Pipp had a headache and couldn't make it that day. The real thing was that Pipp was slowing down and hadn't been hitting, so he just decided that a day's relaxation at the racetrack might help his state of mind and his bankroll. So Wally went to the racetrack that June 2 and Lou Gehrig went to first base.

That was okay for Lou, but otherwise it proved to be a season well worth forgetting for the ball club. The Yankees took a nose dive into seventh place (in an eight-team league), and Babe Ruth went through a series of misadventures that ran the range from his famous "bellyache" to a shouting match in the locker room with Miller Huggins in St. Louis. The little man decided to make an issue of it, so he fined the big man $5,000 and added a suspension. There was nothing meek about the Babe, though. He left the club and flounced off to New York to carry his gripe straight to Jacob Ruppert, the colonel and sportsman who owned the Yankees. Babe even made one of those famous-last-word statements that people make: "It's me or him."

Well, it wasn't Huggins. Afterwards, Ruth became contrite and acted like a little boy who'd been caught with his hand in the cookie jar. And maybe that was his true nature: the little boy with his hand in the cookie jar.

No recollections about Lou Gehrig could leave out recollections of Babe Ruth because they were a "pair" in the lineup, and for a while off the field. But they were as different in their personalities as two men could ever be. The King and the Crown Prince, to trot out one of the names hung on them.

This was the postwar "Golden Age" of sports, and Babe Ruth was the eighteen-carat center of the golden age. A huge, good-natured lummox who called everybody "Kid" or "Joe" because he couldn't remember their real names. The Babe had an incredible flamboyance, with the talent to back it up. Probably the greatest natural baseball player of all time, he was a tremendous outfielder with an arm that set World Series records when he was a pitcher. A smart base-runner with shattering power at the bat. He was the Babe, all right.

Some of the players resented Babe. He was a one-man gang who didn't pay much attention to anybody else's feelings. He was also getting more money than anybody else in baseball, and more than twice as much as anybody else on the Yankees, who weren't famous for the size of their paychecks, anyway. But he was worth every penny of it: He brought in ten extra dollars through the turnstiles for every dollar Ruppert paid him.

Lou admired Babe as a ballplayer. You had to, he was superb. Lou liked him as a man, too, and got a kick out of his shenanigans—even though he didn't want to copy them, and couldn't. I think Babe liked Lou as much as he liked anybody. For a time, they were even roommates. Before that, Babe's roommates had been selected by the team in the hope that they might exert some good influence on him; instead, he exerted some of his own rousing influence on them. No curfew and no set of training rules was invented that could hold Babe down.

If you wonder about that "one-two-punch" business in the batting order, this is what it meant to have Babe and Lou batting in sequence alongside other hitters like Mark Koenig, Bob Meusel and Tony Lazzeri after he'd joined them. In Lou's first full season, 1925, Babe got into only 98 games with all those problems of his and he slumped badly: a .290 batting average with 25 home runs and 66 runs batted in. Lou made the regular lineup that June and finished with a .295 average, plus 20 home runs and 68 runs batted in. Then the Yankees recovered in 1926, and big: Babe hit .372 with 47 homers and 155 runs batted in and Lou averaged .313 with 16 homers and 107 runs batted in, which was a remarkably high figure for only 16 homers. And in 1927, when the Yankees had what was probably the greatest team ever, Ruth hit .356 with 60 home runs and 164 runs batted in and Gehrig hit .373 with 47 homers and 175 runs batted in.

The 1927 Yankees were some baseball team. Lou and Lazzeri and Koenig made up the best young infield in baseball, with the older Joe Dugan at his peak at third base. Ruth, Meusel and Earle Combs were tops in the outfield. The pitching staff had Waite Hoyt, Herb Pennock and George Pipgras, with Wilcy Moore as one of the first and certainly best relief pitchers in the business.

It was the year Ruth set his home-run record of sixty, and he got plenty of support from the fact that he batted No. 3 in the lineup with Gehrig batting No. 4. Whenever Babe went to the plate, the pitcher had two possibilities: walk him or pitch to him. If he chose to pitch, Babe might strike out—or he might knock the ball out of sight. But after Lou started to bat after him, the pitchers faced double jeopardy: If they chose to walk Ruth intentionally, they'd face Gehrig with Ruth on base. They were some pair, particularly that season. Ruth hit all those home runs and Lou was voted the Most Valuable Player in the American League. Between them, they knocked 107 baseballs over fences and knocked in 339 runs.

They even went on a postseason tour that broke attendance records wherever they went, and they kept doing it until the Yankee management called a halt a few years later. By then, Babe and Lou were making more money after the season than during it. And Ruppert wasn't too fond of that development. It made his players a little too independent when they started to talk salary later in the winter.

And that's what Lou had going for him by the time I got off the trolley car from the Century of Progress that afternoon in 1931 and ran into Kitty McHie. "Drop over later for some beer because Lou Gehrig's coming over." Big, handsome, successful, I thought. All those things. And, as luck would have it, painfully shy.

9

Breakfast at the Drake

THE first time I met Lou Gehrig, I was with an escort, who remarked: "That young guy has a great future." The next time I met him, in Kitty McHie's apartment that night, I was alone, but not for long. The "shy one" suddenly became the bold one, singled me out and spent the whole time giving me a shy man's version of the rush.

Kitty noticed what was happening with some amazement, and even warned her other guests to leave us alone. Maybe she knew more than we did. Hadn't she tried to pair us both off to other people before, and failed? This was an unscheduled miracle to her now, and in her own living room.

Kitty then was Mrs. Emory Perry, and she was doing

all right. Her husband had been making a fortune in a tame way, at least for Chicago at the close of the twenties: He was the new king of the plumbing gimmicks—fancy shower curtains with toilet seats to match. No kidding.

The only flaw in the script was that Lou Gehrig was the straightest guy around, with a midnight curfew of his own whenever the Yankees were traveling. I think we were falling slightly in love that night, but I was no match for his curfew. I even started to leave before he turned into a pumpkin or something, but he rose to the occasion by asking if he could show me home. He did, but I was still no match for his Code of Conduct. A block away, at the door of my apartment he abruptly said good-night and disappeared into the dark.

About a week later, just when any red-blooded girl might be wondering if she'd lost the zip on her fastball, the postman rang the bell an unusually long time and then shouted so that all the neighbors would get the message: "Package down here from Lou Gehrig."

It was some package: a diamond cut-crystal necklace that Lou had bought in Japan during one of his baseball tours the year before. That much I got from the note that he'd attached. Now here he was breaking more records for restrained behavior: taking the girl home, not even working up a good-night kiss, and a week later sending her jewels. That was worth a fast phone call to Kitty, who promptly advised: "Send him the sweetest thank-you note you can—immediately. That thing represents the Taj Mahal to him."

I did, and he answered, and I answered the answer.

And, just like that, we started to spiral gently into the sweet expectation that leads to—what? It was hard to measure it in terms of the past, because I'd actually met Lou four years earlier while sitting in the White Sox ball park with Dorothy Grabiner. I'd never particularly been a reader of the sports pages, but we went to baseball games because it was the Thing To Do: You might see a home run go out of the stadium, and in those days that was the main event. Otherwise, I would occasionally drop by Stagg Field to sit alone in the snow and watch the University of Chicago team play football (before Robert M. Hutchins, the chancellor, decided to separate the school from the exaggerated values of its football program). But mostly I was too occupied.

We never dated ballplayers then, probably because there was a caste system and I was part of it. Players never mingled with the office people like the Grabiners—and I was with them. Even years later I caused a few eyebrows to be raised by hobnobbing with the Ed Barrows when they were running the Yankees, though we took great pains to observe the rigors of the caste system, outwardly, at least. The Barrows lived in Larchmont when we were living in New Rochelle, and I would let them drive me to Yankee Stadium in their big green Cadillac—but I'd get out a block from the park and later appear inside by myself to join the other players' wives.

So the Grabiners, in the late twenties, kept their distance, too. In the players' minds, I was supposed to be a millionaire or something; at least, part of the "other" caste. Even when the lordly Yankees came to Chicago with their own millionaires. And if that hadn't worked, then Lou Gehrig's own "caste system" would have kept us apart. He was already established as a star, but he was really an island, and a shy one, at that.

Not only that, but I even joined the fans in rooting against the Yankees, who were always hell-bent for another pennant and who were always getting most of their push from Ruth and Gehrig. Then suddenly that night in Kitty Emory's penthouse, there was the shy one asking if he could fetch me a plate of goodies or a drink, and there we were a few days later exchanging little notes and drifting toward the only "caste system" that mattered, our own.

The notes were fairly noncommittal for a couple of people who already were taken with each other. He didn't bother to tell me that he was going to Rye Beach amusement park every night when the Yankees were home, buying a fistful of tickets for the roller coaster to get his "highs" and his "lows" by himself. And I didn't tell him that my boyfriends were suddenly looking small by comparison. We hadn't begun to confide in each other, at least not just yet.

How's that for playing it straight? But we did, all that fall and winter and the following spring while the Yankees chased south and then chased back north, and finally west when the new season opened. By now, I was beginning to realize that I didn't have the faintest idea how to break down this fantastically reserved character. It was like a problem in riding a horse: a loose rein for a tender mouth, with just the slightest pull on the reins for signals or the beast would bolt.

We met at the Shoreland Hotel for dinner after the Yankees reached town for the first time the next spring. A family hotel, at that. And after several pleasant hours there, it was the old curfew time again, and my shy guy said good-night all around and disappeared for his hotel. My girl friends, who'd been with us, were as dazzled by all this hesitation as their boyfriends.

"He couldn't take his eyes off you," I was advised, as if I needed advice.

"It's a good thing you circulated, he watched every man you talked to."

"Touch his arm, take him over to the window, say the lake is beautiful."

"Call him. Say you just wanted to say good-night. Get your voice low and seductive."

"For God's sake, do *something*."

A few of the men were especially helpful, contributing an "I dare you" to the babel. And so I took them up on it. At two o'clock in the morning, I asked for his room at the Yankees' hotel, and I didn't have the slightest doubt that operators at both ends of the telephone were straining on every syllable.

"I just wanted to say good-night, dear," I offered, eyes narrowing neatly and voice pitched perfectly for effect.

"For Chrissake," the fuzzy voice answered, "do you know what time it is?"

I knew what time it was, all right. Time to hang up,

which we both did. First time I ever called a man like that
and now, one crystal necklace and some friendly letters
later, I'd become a "baseball Annie" in his eyes. Fallen
woman, New York Yankee style.

I had no laurels to sleep on, and didn't. So I got up
early and went to work, grateful for my job as secretary at
the Century of Progress. And, whatever blunders I might
perpetrate after hours, that was about as high as a girl
could climb in those days. So this was it; spinsterhood and
alarm clocks.

But life is stranger than soap operas. After I arrived at
the office, I glanced out the window and guessed that I
wasn't the only one who hadn't done much slumbering.
There was Lou down on the street, making wild motions
in the direction of my window, motioning me with open
arms and that mile-wide grin. I did a double-take and raced
downstairs and then, in front of the whole Century of
Progress staff arriving for work, we kissed madly in the
center of Grant Park.

We went to the Drake Hotel for breakfast. I don't remember who proposed to whom. We just plotted and
planned. Everything, including the fact that his "Mom
would be hard to handle," and so we even created a strategy of sorts for *that* problem. We lingered over coffee for
hours, then drove to my house to tackle whatever problems we'd find there. There weren't any, unless you count
my mother's tears, but they were happy ones. Everybody
was so happy, in fact, that we damned near forgot about
the ball game he was supposed to play that afternoon. So I
called my office, made some meaningless excuse and

headed for Comiskey Park with him. By then, the news-papers had been tipped off and we were surrounded by photographers, though we stopped short of admitting that it was official. Did he hit a home run? You bet your life he hit a home run, strictly following the script in the corniest way imaginable.

Baseball's a nomad's game, though, and two days later the Yankees moved on to St. Louis. But, we were insepa-rable during those two days in Chicago. Lou ate his meals at our house and went back to his hotel only long enough to sleep. The old curfew again. We came clean with only two of the Yankees: the new manager, Joe McCarthy, and Lou's roommate, Bill Dickey. But in the history of peo-ple's personal secrets, I would have to say that this one didn't rate too high. Somehow, it even got back to his mother in the family fortress in New Rochelle.

I hadn't had very much experience with mothers-in-law, so at Lou's suggestion I invited Mrs. Gehrig to be my guest in Chicago. And she came. It was one of those times for all good women to come to the aid of the party, and they did. Kitty even took her in as a houseguest for a few days. It wasn't easy, because she started to nitpick early and often. Maybe it was the contrast with my own mother, who'd always been close to my friends—in age and affection. They all called my mom "Nel," and so did I, affectionately. But Lou's mother had other ideas; she thought that "Nel" business was outrageous, for one thing. She also was turned off when we took her to a smart, private supper club (courtesy of Harry Grabiner's membership card) and she wasn't charmed, either, when

Sophie Tucker came over to our table after her songs and put her arms around Mrs. Gehrig. The best way I can put it is that she lacked humor or ease to an alarming degree.

I know that I had my hands full trying to entertain her, future mother-in-law or not. When she finally left town a few days later, my friends and I were worn out. I wrote Lou a long letter and laid it on the line: It wouldn't be easy. But Lou hastened to reassure me, and begged me to stick with him.

This was becoming a good old-fashioned triangle—me, my man and my man's mother—and the contrasts were heightened by the fact that we had all reached that point in place and time by extremely different paths. Lou had just started to escape from the apron strings; I had never particularly been tied to any; but there was his mother, strenuously fighting to preserve all the ties that bind. Classic case, classic dilemma.

We tried a lot of solutions and we tried to tread softly while finding the solutions; that's how much Lou and I wanted to make our new-found love work. We decided that I would leave Chicago for New York as soon as possible, to find an apartment in a suburb close to Mrs. Gehrig—to make the "parting" of mother and son less sorrowful, if you can appreciate that. Two things were embroiling her, it developed: Lou had already told her that from the day of his marriage, his wife would come first, and he had passed the word that we positively were determined to get our own apartment and not double-up with the Gehrigs.

To get the full picture, you have to turn your own clock back a couple of generations, back to the days when courtship and marriage tended to rise or fall on such domestic involvements. Then, if the picture still doesn't come into focus, consider all the little subplots in our private drama. Like this one: Before I left Chicago, there was one Sunday night when Lou didn't telephone me at the "usual" time. By eleven o'clock, I was a wreck. So I called him instead, and got no answer. Finally at midnight Lou got through to me and *whispered* that he had taken his mother to see *The Silver Cord* by Sidney Howard. It was a strong drama about a domineering mother and the havoc she causes to her son's marriage; a fairly heavy dose to give the poor old soul. But at the same time, it was reassuring to learn that Lou also understood the depth of the problem we faced.

Early that September, I gave my boss notice, lined up a good replacement for him as a going-away present and shipped most of my mother's stunning furniture to a warehouse in New Rochelle. That was part of the picture, too: *my* mother was taking a smaller apartment in Chicago and we were inheriting some of her furniture while I was gathering myself for the battle of the mother-in-law. So I headed east for Round One.

The idea was that I'd stay with the Gehrigs while hunting for an apartment for Lou and myself. I wasn't looking forward to seeing Mom Gehrig, let alone playing the role of "the other woman" in her lifelong battle for her son's mind and attention. She betrayed an awkward, even blundering resentment at every step. But my game was passive resistance, avoiding any direct confrontation with her, and I found that I also had a strong and resolute man behind me: her son.

I came up with a small apartment in New Rochelle not far from Lou's home. No great trick, because the Depression created lots of vacancies. So now the problem was narrowing down to the basics—getting married and moving in, without rocking the boat too steeply.

We are talking about a formidable person when we're talking about Lou's mother, not just a mild irritant to a spoiled girl who had led a carefree life until running into the Gehrigs' iron fence. Formidable, built something like a lady wrestler, with yellowish gray hair snatched back in a bun. No hairdresser for her, certainly no makeup. Not that it would have mattered anyway, since she was in a state of steaming perpetual motion, no idle hands, chores around the clock. A huge breakfast to be prepared for her husband and son, then an attack on the sinkful of dishes, then an almost compulsive session with the vegetables and meat for the night's dinner.

Finally, she would jam a hat on her head and leave for Yankee Stadium *with* Lou, in time for batting practice. Afterwards, back in the kitchen while Pop walked the dogs again and the parrot kept shouting baseball lingo

---

I just wanted him to develop his capacity for enjoying life and for identifying with some of the better things in it. And Lou graduated from "B" pictures—and golf, skating and fishing—to the theater, to opera, to Toscanini, even to the ballet.

Wide World

Some people thought Lou was jealous because Babe Ruth was No. 1 with the public and with the paymaster, but that was nonsense. He always idolized Ruth as a baseball player loaded with talent.

It started like an old-fashioned triangle—me, my man, and my man's mother. His father, Henry, was a leaf-hammerer, a man who pounded patterns into sheets of metal. His mother, Christina, had a fixation to keep the family together and to make something of her son. (Associated Press Photo)

He had been the regular first-baseman for the Yankees since June 1, 1925, and every day when he jogged out to first base, Luke added another game to his own strange record for playing without a break. . . .

until he was covered for the night. And at last the evening meal, starting with caviar on toast, thick soup, a Caesar salad, meat, potatoes, the vegetables, oversized dessert, the whole works. In the backwash of this way of life, several maids came and went as members of the cast; they simply got in the way of the steamroller.

After dinner and the dishes, we would settle in the living room. Mom would grab either the crochet or knitting bag and get her fingers flying, uttering sage little philosophies like "what goes up must come down," and Pop would invariably nod in agreement. Sometimes a glint would creep into her steel-blue eyes, and I'd swear she was figuring out how to "acquire" me as a part-time maid and full-time playmate for her son.

I remember the night I decided the hell with it all. I got up from my chair and signaled Lou to follow me. When we got to the kitchen, I whispered that I was leaving as soon as his parents had gone to bed for the night. He began to plead, and that goaded me even more. Finally, I quieted down and we returned to the living room to wait them out until they quit for the evening. When they did, I sneaked upstairs to pack, he made a dash for the car, and hustled down the driveway and gave it the gun. A block beyond, I broke our engagement. He cried; I cried; everybody cried. At least until we boarded the ferry.

In those days, you could avoid all kinds of traffic by taking the ferry from Westchester County across Long Island Sound. It was a neat idea, particularly with an accordion player and a violinist to serenade the passengers. Of course, they were playing "our song" that night, and of course I broke down and we got engaged again. But I stuck to my guns as far as the immediate issue went—staying in Mom Gehrig's private fortress—and he agreed to take me to Long Island and the home of my Uncle Gene and Aunt Blanche Austin.

When we arrived, I think Lou saw the beauty of the idea, too. It was so happy there, with Gene and Blanche living it up. They were so loose that they thought we'd just dropped by on a lark of some kind, making some last-minute plans for the wedding. We explained our troubles, and they just asked me to transfer my headquarters there. My mother and brother were scheduled to arrive soon for the wedding, anyway; the caterer was making plans, the guests had been invited. My own feeling was that I needed as many bodies around me as possible.

Sometimes I got my wish in strange ways, and in very public ways—which was the other side of the coin. Since coming east from Chicago to tie the knot, most of my anxiety had been centered on the people and the problems inside the Gehrig household, especially the ultimate problem of relating myself to the life and customs of Lou's old-world parents. I still hadn't come into close contact with the people or problems *outside* that household, out there where I'd be spending the rest of our life together.

My first clue to *that* side of things came one day when it rained, the Yankees got the day off and Lou came over to Blanche's house early. That's when she came up with the perfect rainy-day idea: Why not spend the day in some-place like Macy's basement getting together some of the things we were going to need when we got down to the really practical, bread-and-butter chores of keeping our own house—like kitchen utensils? We had not yet come down to earth long enough to think about little items like knives and forks. So the three of us drove into town, parked the car and headed into Macy's basement.

I got my wish, all right. We had just about entered the place when we were surrounded by bodies, dozens of them drawing a bead on the one and only Lou Gehrig as he walked the aisles of the store hunting bargains in spoons. It turned into a mob scene with Twitchell in the middle of the mob being tossed around pretty briskly, until Lou did what any red-blooded American boy would do under those pressing circumstances: He turned and got the hell out of there. Straight into the men's room. So Blanche and I pulled ourselves together while the mob dispersed, got our hair patted down, and started buying things left and right while Mr. Hero languished in the john. We finally rescued him and drove him home.

And now I had the "tools" of the trade. All I needed after that was some tips on how to use them. But we already had included that in our sweeps along the counters—one large, easy to comprehend cook book.

The day before the wedding, I was in my new apartment in New Rochelle with Blanche and my mother; we were surrounded by all the furniture that had been delivered and piled high on the floor. It was early in the morning. The carpet-layers were scheduled to arrive anytime. We all put on aprons, we all got to work sorting out the stuff, plumbers came and plumbers went, our new janitor got to work, the new telephone was installed. You get the picture; it was a typical day-before-the-wedding mess.

Suddenly, Lou came rushing in and tossed a bomb into the middle of the mess. His mother was raising hell or had gone berserk, or something resembling both states of mind. And this time, he didn't fumble the ball. He picked up the new phone, called the mayor of New Rochelle, and told him to bring the marriage license and make it fast. A little while later, the mayor did exactly that, to the accompaniment of a covey of motorcycle cops escorting him.

So the classiest wedding ever held in Westchester County, New York, began to take shape in the debris. The carpet-layers, the plumbers, the janitor, the cops, the coatless groom, the besmudged bride and the aproned attendants all stood rigid—at strict military attention, frozen in place—while Mayor Otto intoned the words that made this unlikely looking couple man and wife. One day early.

A case of champagne had been delivered a few days before as a wedding gift, so the janitor scurried around for some ice, after which improperly cooled champagne was served all around.

So, as they say, we were married. Ignoring the nice elaborate plans we had made for the same wedding the next day on Long Island before family and friends. Skipping the timetable we had so carefully arranged since that day we had proposed to each other in Grant Park or at the Drake Hotel, or wherever it was. Thumbing our noses at the old baseball manager's axiom that a player began to lose his vitality once he'd taken the fatal step—even

There was no particular reason to keep playing without a break, no particular compulsion—except the fascination of adding one more day, one more week, whatever you lost.

Wide World Photos

Culver Pictures, Inc.

155

though Bill Dickey, Lyn Lary, Lefty Gomez and Babe Ruth among the Yankees all had married great-looking showgirl types. And we'd done it all to escape from the heavy hand of the guy's mother.

We also had done it "early" from the baseball point of view. Originally, we had conceded the point about not mixing marriage with the American League schedule. We did that by planning the ceremony for the day after the season ended. But now we'd taken the plunge with that one final game remaining to be played, and we cheerfully paid the price for that switch. I had some clothes in the closet in New Rochelle and I made a quick change of costume. Then we sort of raced down to the stadium with a motorcycle escort (Mayor Otto's boys) with sirens whining. On my golden wedding day.

When we walked into our little apartment that night, it was in perfect order—for a change. The champagne was chilled by now, and there were two cold lobsters sitting on ice. Our gang of wedding attendants had labored, then had disappeared like elves. Like elves who had cleaned up the royal mess while the young couple was busy escaping the clutches of the ancient curse. They did nobly, too, those janitors and plumbers and carpet-layers and just plain elves.

We paid another price for the right to our fairy tale. Lou's mother had always harped on the financial hardship she might have to endure when he started to live with that "other" woman, namely me. So, to cover the cost of his "divorce" from the apron strings, Lou put every cent he'd saved up to that time into trust for her. His mother and fa-

ther were to get the income for life, while we were to control any changes in the investments, it added up to a
monthly income for them of slightly over $200, and in
those days that wasn't hay. In addition, Lou gave his
parents the keys to a new car and the deed to their house.
The money would revert to us on their deaths. All that
was fine with me. As for the lovers? We started from
scratch—but, at least we started.

We had a few things going for us besides those beautiful
feelings. I had a fine trousseau. Lou salvaged one suit,
though he refused to "go back" to the house for the rest of
his belongings. We were too broke to even think of going
on a honeymoon. We broke all the rigid old rules that
would've run our life if we hadn't staged our little revolt:
We ate when we got hungry, we got up or down when we
pleased. Lou helped with the housework. We did the gro-
cery shopping together. We went fishing, we took in
shows, we got to know each other. I inveigled him into
Abercrombie & Fitch, barricaded him into a fitting
room, got the floor manager to take charge and to quote
the prices at half-strength as part of the strategy and then I
watched while they carted in armfuls of sports coats,
slacks, shirts and sweaters.

The beautiful slob became a peacock before my eyes,
and he loved every minute of it. The bride made sure that
everything fitted that magnificent physique to a "T." He
couldn't quite get over the notion of how reasonably
priced it all was, but he didn't resist when I gave an airy
wave of the hand and instructed them to "charge and send
it" to our new home.

Our new home. And it was there that he cemented our courtship, wedding, revolt and life together in one instinctive gesture, tossing the checkbook onto the desk and saying: "Our old age is in your hands, Eleanor."

Not right now, baby, I thought. Not right now.

10

———⁓———

Life with Luke

T HE known facts were these: It was the fall of 1933, the country was mired in the Depression, signs were appearing in store windows with the initials "N.R.A." for Roosevelt's National Recovery Act, some of the young ones in the army of out-of-work were going to work in the Civilian Conservation Corps camps, Hitler was consolidating his power moves inside Germany. All of that, though, seemed safely in the background as my man—my "Luke" is what I called him—and I settled into the apartment at 5 Circuit Road in New Rochelle, at the corner of the Boston Post Road, sort of around the corner from his parents' place at 9 Meadow Lane.

They were the happiest days of my life, and that was

one of the known facts, too. The unknown fact was that they would last just six years.

There were adjustments, of course, because we had come from contrasting backgrounds and had contrasting tastes. But Luke solved the biggest adjustment of all, the classic wife-mother confrontation, by rising to the occasion and announcing to his strong-willed mother: "Eleanor will come first." It was that direct and that decisive; afterwards, she and I got along fine in a kind of truce dictated by our differing claims on the man we loved.

Another major adjustment was strictly between Lou and me: finding, discovering, learning and fitting into each other's worlds. And that adjustment became a way of life, not too far removed from the way of life that other couples grope for and reach in their own way, with their own results. I was no "society girl," whatever the newspapers said in their flights of fancy; but I had grown up with more involvement in "society" than Lou Gehrig, just as he had matured in the physical world of professional sports, ballplayers, reporters, columnists and the characters who surround them all.

He also was addicted to easy little pastimes like western movies, and for a while he suffered through his own tug-of-war on that. I remember that a month or so after we were married he announced after dinner one night that he was going to the neighborhood movie house to "take in" the cowboy picture. He didn't invite me to go along, but just halfheartedly shuffled out the door. For a minute or two, I was puzzled by his change of pace, but I figured it wasn't that he wanted to see the picture so much—it was more that he wanted to establish the point, in a small boy's way, that he was his own man.

He was beautiful: 6 feet tall, 205 pounds strong, sturdy as a rock and innocent as a waif. Half an hour later, he was back inside the apartment with a sheepish look on his squared face. I don't know why I pulled that little stunt, so go ahead and unload the works on me.

In my mind, as the observer of this little subplot, I guessed that he'd gotten a few lampposts away from the house and then stopped to ask himself what he'd been trying to prove in the first place. He answered it in one word—nothing—and was honest enough with himself to skip the whole thing. So he came home. I'm no psychologist, and never was one, but I knew enough about human nature not to lord it over him. I just broke the short silence by asking why he hadn't brought back the evening paper. He took the opening like a flash, shooting out the door and hustling back in a few minutes with the evening paper. Relaxed, happy, reprieved.

But it wasn't always a one-way street when it came to adjusting our foibles and our worlds. We'd been married on the last day of the baseball season, and a few weeks later it was my turn. The big fish were running off Long Island, and we were invited to do some deep-sea fishing by Fred Fletcher, one of Lou's friends, who was the rod-and-gun editor of the *New York Daily News*. Actually, I had been expecting some initiation into Lou's circle of activity, so I realized that his interest in deep-sea fishing wasn't

simply a matter of putting a worm on a hook and dropping
the line over the side of a rowboat. And don't forget, I'm
from the Midwest.

Off we went at four in the morning, which was one instant adjustment I had to make; then the long, cold drive
from New Rochelle to the tip of Long Island to board the
ship by dawn at Montauk. Fred was already aboard, so we
nosed the boat into the Atlantic for about two hours of
pleasant cruising to the fishing grounds, harnessed into
swivel chairs, heavy fishing gear in our mitted hands, the
captain chatting about where the big ones had been running the day before and the mate cutting hunks of mack-
erel into bait. So far, so good.

Lou kept taking side glances at me, probably because
the sea was choppy and he wasn't taking any chances with
his landlubbing bride. Then the captain cut the engines
down to a gentler speed and now we were what you'd call
trolling. Very peaceful again. Strong coffee brewing in the
galley, a prediction by somebody that breakfast would be
served in an hour. I dozed off, happy, my man beside me,
all adjustments proceeding smoothly.

Then the captain, sitting in his elevated chair at the
wheel scanning the surface, shouted "School!" And everyone sprang to attention as though he'd sighted a subma-
rine. Then a terrific jolting "Wham!" and something big
and strong had grabbed the bait at the long end of the line
attached to me. Now everybody started screaming at me
to let "him" run with the line, then horse "him" in, pump
in, pump out, keep your line taut or he'll spit the bait, and
all of a sudden—way out there many yards into the

water—"he" cleared the surface with a stunning leap and shook in midair like some fury before sliding back beneath the water, still yanking on my hook.

But now nobody in particular was helping me, except to continue yelling instructions too fast and too ridiculous for me to follow. I gave it the old college try, though, even after my arms began to ache about half an hour later. Half an hour later of struggling as though "*he*" had me hooked instead of the other way around. The farther out the creature got, the farther I'd have to drag him back, while the skipper kept maneuvering the boat so that my line wouldn't get snagged underneath.

Twenty times I wanted to beg my chums to "unharness me," but I would have become a disgrace to the East Coast Fishing Club, the New York Yankees and the House of Morgan. So I held on for an hour more, no kidding; horsing him in, letting him out, reeling him in again, until after a few more desperate runs the monster gave up the match.

When I pulled him alongside the boat, the four men who formed my audience and my cheering section turned their full attention on the fish. Affectionate comments like "beautiful," and "outstanding," and "must be over 300 pounds, maybe 350." Then Luke remembered I was still aboard and came over to pat my head, unharness me and light me a cigarette. Then with tenderness and some awe, he led me over to view the catch: a blue-fin tuna, they told me, and I'd have to admit it *was* beautiful. One of the rarer and scrappier creatures in the sea, so they decided on the spot to cut him loose to help keep the breed going.

They patted his belly, cut the line and launched him back toward the spawning grounds with a sore mouth and probably a very bruised disposition as a reminder of his encounter with that bride from Chicago one cool morning in October, 1933.

How's that for getting myself submerged into part of Gehrig's world of the great outdoors? Well, it soon turned too cold for more adventures on the sea and then it was my turn at bat in the adjustment league. The opera season had opened and I wasted no time inviting my man to invite me there. He was trapped this time, but he was game. He made only one stipulation: We'd have to go secretly, if that was possible. He was really being fussy about that, but I got the point: Ballplayers are targets for all kinds of heckling from the guys in the other dugout during the summer and, if it got around the American League that Gehrig had become an opera buff during the winter, he could be totally certain of one thing—every time he went to bat, he'd hear a chorus of the most shrieking off-key arias and yodeling imaginable. Anything to rattle the man going to the plate, so it was agreed that we would make our debut together at the Met by creeping into and out of the opera house as inconspicuously as possible. Don't forget, those were the days when baseball players were pretty rough characters; none of the culture levels you find in the dugout today.

Wagnerian operas were going strong that season, so I picked out *Tristan und Isolde* for Lou's first opera. It runs about four hours and it's a heavy one, so I had some qualms about it for his first visit. I did take the trouble to explain the plot in detail, and that's a lot of detail. I also took out some social insurance so the evening wouldn't be a total loss: I made reservations at "21" for a midnight supper.

First came the prelude, the overture, the low and vibrant tones of the passionate music. And now it was my turn to steal the sidelong glances at the "newcomer," the way he'd done on the boat a few days earlier. He was getting the same reaction, too. Nice and peaceful, no problems. Then the curtain lifted, a ravishing Isolde appeared, also Tristan, and after that the place began to fill with majestic music. That did it. Lou sat bolt upright, the way I'd sat while fighting his magnificent fish, and this time *he* was hooked. Just like that, he identified for the first time in his life with grand opera.

He identified even more during the following scenes; even to the point of getting moist around the eyes. By the end of the final act and its love-death duet, he was an emotional wreck.

One reason for his involvement was that he could follow every heroic word and phrase in German. So the next thing I knew, he was living opera and loving it, and he also was dragging me to the opera house all winter. He even bought the librettos to all the operas that season and, during the Saturday afternoon radio broadcasts from the Metropolitan, there was old Luke sprawled on the floor following the melodrama, note by note, line by line.

So he discovered my world of opera and literature, and I discovered him. I discovered that this was no automaton, no unfeeling giant. A sensitive and even soft man who wept while I read him *Anna Karenina* and other classics. The experiences were new to him, but the feelings had been deep inside him waiting for the masterwork that might bring them out. That's the way he was—anything he loved, he embraced to the point of tears, and it was that way in every direction he turned.

For example, he wasn't just grateful to his parents for their sacrifices; he was grateful with a passion. On the ball field, he wasn't just dedicated; he was fanatical. In anything he came into contact with, he was hungry for the knowledge and the *savoir-faire* that many people doubted he could grasp. So he wasn't simply the strong, silent type; he was vulnerable, easily hurt, quickly cut. So much so that when he thought he had treated me brusquely, he'd go around the house and refuse to talk to me for what seemed like hours. By then, I was thoroughly rattled and wondering what I had done to *him*. I am not the silent type, and I would soon be begging for his forgiveness for whatever I might have done, real or imagined. But then, it would turn out that he really had been suffering through a little spell of self-rebuke, exiling himself and not me, sulking at his own moodiness.

What he needed badly was confidence, building up; he was absolutely anemic for kindness and warmth. He had never known closeness or close love before, and when he found it, he grew frightened to death that he might lose it. So he needed constant reassurance, and I'd prop him up again and again, until his next sinking spell. This was my man, maybe my man-child, Luke.

So our first winter went on, from one stepping-stone to

another, crossing personal or social bridges with each other. Lou graduated from "B" pictures to the Broadway theater, to opera, to Toscanini, even to the ballet. He decided that ballet dancers were the best-trained athletes of all. Actors and actresses in turn took an instant shine to him, probably because there is a kinship between professional athletes and professional actors: A hit show one year, a flop the next, audience reaction, public adulation or reproach, new names skyrocketing to fame—and only a few performers holding center stage for long.

We talked a lot about this during those first months together. He knew I wasn't leading him into a madcap life; he also knew I didn't want a dilettante on my hands. I just wanted him to develop his capacity for enjoying life and for identifying with some of the better things in it. We were partners, it was that simple.

We had planned on his retiring from baseball when he reached thirty-five, and he was already thirty. But he promised that, even if he was still doing terrifically well in baseball by then, he would still call it quits on the target date. I swore that I would never live through the spectacle or the ordeal of a fading athlete who was traded from one team to another, his price tag declining, sale merchandise on aching legs and muscles. An athlete usually is an old man professionally at thirty-five; even at thirty, he was being described in the newspapers as "the veteran first baseman." So we made our pact. He would retire at thirty-five and then perhaps discover that an old ballplayer can emerge into private life as still a young man.

Besides, there were no baseball pensions in those days.

1934: We headed for the Orient with an all-star ball team that was gently commanded by Connie Mack and crammed with talent like Lefty O'Doul, Jimmy Foxx, Lefty Gomez, Babe Ruth, Charley Gehringer, Earl Averill—and Lou Gehrig. . . .

. . . Lou and I returned by way of Singapore, Bombay, Cairo, Rome, Munich, Paris, and London, living on the edge of the earthquake that was gathering around Europe and the world.

You played, if you were lucky, and you left when they found somebody else younger and stronger. It's a business, we accepted that. To the fans, it probably seems like fun and games, though that notion may have changed now with all the emphasis on long-term contracts and security. In the 1930s, though, there were few comforts in "tomorrow" for the ballplayer; he had to make it "today" or not at all. We also realized that a "name" player was most likely to be traded just before he began to show signs of wear, when he was still marketable, I'd guess you'd say. He can be exchanged then for two or three young players, maybe even enough cash to bail out a weak franchise. He is told to report to his new employer the next day, and he reports. In that respect, Lou stayed lucky—he'd been born in New York and he played ball in New York. But even though he had that certain "star quality" and the rank that went with it, we always knew that it was a business built on variables and we promised ourselves that we would eliminate those variables when he turned thirty-five.

Then it was 1934 and we were getting ready for my next "experience" as the baseball bride: spring training in St. Petersburg, Florida. We left early so that Lou could get in some more fishing off the Florida Keys before reporting to the Yankee camp and to Joe McCarthy, who three years before had replaced Bob Shawkey, the interim successor to Miller Huggins, the Mighty Midget, who had passed away. The Yankees were still on top of the heap more often than not—champions in 1927 with 110 victories (in 154 games), champions again in 1928 with 101 victories, then second or third for three years before winning it all again in 1932. After that, they ran second three years in a row while the team graduated from the era of Babe Ruth to the days of Joe DiMaggio, with Gehrig forming the bridge to the past.

Spring training was a pleasurable time then, especially if you had last year's prize money still in your pockets. We stopped off at Miami that spring and had dinner with Mrs. Jimmy Walker, the wife of the former mayor of New York. While there, we put in a call to Blanche and Gene Austin in New Orleans, where they were spending the winter. It turned out to be a fateful call: They had been trying to find me because my father had suffered a stroke and was dying. So there was nothing for me to do but take the next train to New Orleans while Lou went on to camp minus his new bride.

My father was still conscious when I arrived two days later, and we had a short talk. A few hours later, he sank into a coma and the next day he died. We buried him in his favorite town in a little French cemetery, the town where he had started so many years earlier. I settled his affairs, then began the long trip back to Florida, finally making my first training camp a week late and again surrounded by the realities of life in the middle of that otherwise relaxed and happy scene.

You are like a gypsy in baseball. You set up your home in New Rochelle for the winter and you leave it in February for the South. When the team heads north, you hit the trail home and finally you go through the summer in two-week intervals of saying hello and good-bye to your husband. You may be paid well for your trouble, but you spend well, too; and after a while, as enjoyable as the traveling around may be, you begin to long for some straight and uninterrupted time back home.

It was all new to me that February when I joined Lou in St. Petersburg, a city on the Gulf of Mexico that even then was a haven for older people. A sunny place where the street crossings are graded so that wheelchairs can be rolled onto the sidewalks, which are lined with green benches so that people can rest their old bones while waiting for the bus or walking slowly from the department stores to the boardinghouses and hotels downtown. A place where shuffleboard gets a big play alongside baseball, the spring sport.

When I checked into the Yankees' hotel, many a gray head peered over the top of a newspaper to get a look at the new girl in town. But I stepped briskly to the desk to sign in, alongside a dapper and distinguished-looking old gentleman. Out of the corner of my eye, I recognized him: he was Colonel Jacob Ruppert, the bachelor sportsman, brewery heir and owner of the Yankees. But I skipped the chance to start at the top socially. I was a "new" Yankee, and I just hurried to my room and my lover for the new lease on life that finally was arriving.

Lou was always in great physical shape, so spring training was no great hardship for him. My first trip to training camp proved to be no great hardship for me. I met all the players and their wives, the club's executives and the swarms of newspaper writers assigned to keep the day-to-day chronicle of the New York Yankees. New York had many newspapers in those days, and baseball had very little competition from basketball or hockey or football, so the ball teams were always accompanied by an army of reporters and columnists from February to October. So everything got off to a fine start except for one thing; the Gehrigs weren't speaking to the Ruths.

There have been a lot of rumors and speculation about Lou and Babe and their gut feeling for each other. Some people thought Lou was jealous because Babe was No. 1 with the public and with the paymaster, but that was nonsense—Gehrig was a wide-eyed rookie when Ruth was the established star of the team and of the game, and Lou always idolized Ruth as a baseball player who was loaded with talent. Others thought that Ruth resented the fact that they were opposites and that people ranked Lou as the virtuous crown prince of the team. But that was nonsense, too.

What happened was a lot more human that that. Babe Ruth had been estranged from his first wife, who later died in a fire. By the time I became one of the Yankee wives, he had married Claire Hodgson, a good-looking widow from Georgia who had a young daughter—as did Babe, who had adopted a daughter, named Dorothy, during his first marriage. So overnight, the big man became a husband and father presiding over a huge apartment on Riverside Drive, which was fine with the Yankee brass— who regarded any such commitment as a possible harness on Babe's normally high spirits.

At that point, Babe was still a favorite in Mom Gehrig's house, though his visits there had changed since his earlier forays at the dining table in the days when she was chief

What I meant was: I can't get to first base *without* you.

cook and hostess to the hungry Yankees. The strain came when Babe and Claire took a trip once, leaving Babe's daughter with a maid at home. Dorothy then paid a visit to the Gehrigs' house in New Rochelle and Lou's mother, in her somewhat heavy manner, decided that the child had been "left" home somewhat shabbily dressed and maybe even neglected, at least for one of the royal princesses of baseball. When Babe and Claire returned to pick her up, there was an exchange of words that may have started as repartee but quickly deteriorated into some catcalling. Claire resented the implication, gathered up Dorothy and left under steam.

So when I made my first appearance in the Yankees' training base, it was a Hatfield-and-McCoy situation. It was a real strain that kept Lou and Babe silent with each other, and I walked right into the silence. There was no showdown or anything like that, because the Ruths were allowed to live in a remote part of town during spring training. But I inherited the problem when I inherited Lou's relationships with the Yankees.

As for the mighty Bambino, I saw him only on the playing field then. He seemed to me to be a pot-bellied, spindly-legged, good-natured buffoon. But he was clearly the big man when it came to baseball, or to anything else, for that matter. There was no whispering about him, because he did everything out in the open. He loved the bottle, he loved to eat, he was an uncommon ladies' man when he was unattached, and he was absolutely tremendous at bat and in the field. You had to look at him and feel that you were watching one of the wonders of the world.

The management did all sorts of things to restrain the Babe. They even discreetly suggested that the new Mrs. Ruth accompany him on all road trips at the club's expense, and that was a revolution in the social and economic history of baseball. She agreed, though it meant long trips by train (in a private compartment in their case), changing towns every three or four days, packing and unpacking in hotel rooms without air conditioning. But she did it, and she exerted a sobering effect on him, no pun intended.

Once Jimmy Walker even berated Babe at a public dinner for setting a bad example for kids, and Ruth reacted by crying over the suggestion that he had let people down. But that's the way he was: riding high until somebody muttered, then deflated and hurt to tears. A huge man and a small child combined in one runaway personality. And he was destined to be humiliated at the end of his career, too, when he let himself be trotted around as a "player-coach" with the Boston Braves after he and the Yankees had parted. Which was one reason, long before people had bungled Babe Ruth's retirement or banishment or whatever you might call it, that Lou and I decided on pulling out of baseball when Lou reached thirty-five. We didn't want any tragic mistakes clouding the close of Gehrig's career.

In the spring of 1934, Ruth had just turned thirty-nine, but the summer before that he had batted .301 with 34 home runs and he had knocked in 103 runs. It was his twentieth season in the big leagues. Lou was thirty, going on thirty-one, and he was starting his tenth full season. The summer before, he had hit .334 with 32 home runs and had driven in 139 runs. They were still playing alongside some of the men from the old Murderers' Row of the late twenties, like Earl Combs, Tony Lazzeri and Bill Dickey. And they were still something.

Then, after six weeks in the sun, we broke camp and headed north. The Yankees meandered up the coast by barnstorming through the cities and towns along the route, the wives kissing them good-bye and driving in different directions to homes across the country. I packed my bags and started the long drive to New York alone, through Florida, Georgia and the Carolinas. Ballplayers usually buy homes in their own towns, or at least they used to; and it was amusing to be driving along and see road markers reading "Home of Carl Hubbell" or "Ty Cobb Lived Here." I could have had free drinks all the way north if I'd introduced myself in the local pubs, but I stuck to the wheel, happy in the new life I'd found, mulling over the strange summer shaping up in New York and thinking beyond that to the tour of Japan that was being talked about by some of the Yankees.

In 1936, Joe DiMaggio arrived from San Francisco of the Pacific Coast League and the Yankees began another phase of their long reign, taking four straight pennants and the World Series. Lou hit .354 with 49 home runs, batted in 152 runs, and was voted the Most Valuable Player in the American League.

I reached New York ahead of the team and slipped right into my new role: baseball wife. My mother had taken her nest egg and rented a small apartment in the Bronx, so she was only half an hour away from me now. Then on opening day in April, I drove to Yankee Stadium for my "debut" with Lou alongside me in the car. I dropped him at the clubhouse door, parked the car in the "official" lot across the street, then discovered that I didn't have a ticket to get inside. But I latched on to a scout I'd met in Florida, followed him up a ramp and sat next to him in the mezzanine. Twitchell had arrived in the big leagues.

Before long, I found that my role included a sensitive time after every home game: the drive back home. It was sensitive because the context for the drive home included two possibilities—the Yankees had either won the game or lost it. I was still a rookie in baseball arithmetic then, and it was just as well. I didn't even have to ask him who'd won when he slid into the car next to me. If the Yankees had won, he was normal; if they'd lost, silence for the half-hour ride to New Rochelle. They played 154 games a season and you'd think no one game was that critical; but think again. When the Yankees lost a game, Lou was still playing it all over again through dinner, and I never had the temerity to say something trite like, "Cheer up, kid, it's just another ball game." The piano might have gone out the window.

Lou had so few faults of character that I didn't begrudge him this one. But it was a big one while it lasted. The team was on the road half the summer but, counting the days at home when they lost games, I was slowly becoming the victim of an occupational disease.

As luck would have it, the Yankees won ninety-four times that summer, lost sixty times and finished second to the Detroit Tigers. Then my freshman year was over and my sometimes-silent man came home for good chattering about something called "the Triple Crown." I tried to look pleased, but all I could envision was some gaudy bejeweled tiara being placed on my head. Lou was patient about it, explaining that it meant he had swept the arithmetic at bat: most home runs (49), most runs batted in (165) and highest batting average (.363). Most Valuable Player in the American League, besides.

So Lou was properly jubilant, more so when he realized that I'd prepared a special private dinner to celebrate. But I was celebrating something else in baseball arithmetic: the end of *my* first season in the American League, with no disasters for my man, and the end of my first year as his wife. It was our first wedding anniversary and—hits, runs and errors aside—that was reason enough for jubilation by the rookie Mrs. Luke.

11

$\smile$

A Game in the
Scheme of Things

So in the gathering autumn of 1934, we were the only couple in the world with something called baseball's Triple Crown and with two loaded trunks in the living room. The trunks were ready to go out the front door in the morning, which they did, bound for the liner Empress of Japan at Vancouver—and a few days later, we chased after them and after the busy, brief days of this new life together.

We were headed for a tour of the Orient with an "all-star" ball team that was gently commanded by Connie Mack of the Philadelphia Athletics. The team was so crammed with talent that you should properly drop the quotation marks from "all-star." Besides the manager, who was addressed as "Mr. Mack" by just about everybody in sight, we were joined by Frank "Lefty" O'Doul and his wife from San Francisco, Jimmie Foxx and his wife from Philadelphia, Vernon "Lefty" Gomez and his wife from New York, and Babe Ruth and his wife from Riverside Drive.

There were plenty of others, too, but my man and I were still lost in each other as we headed for Chicago on board the Twentieth-Century Limited. For the junior members of the audience, the Twentieth Century was an elegant train that was named for the one thing in our lives then that instantly reminded people that we belonged to an enlightened civilization. Scientifically enlightened, anyway. And that was our twentieth century, then in its fourth decade surrounded by mechanical marvels and political storms, and before long the mechanical marvels would combine with the political storms to produce another cataclysmic war.

But there we were, holding back the tide with our own bubbling emotions, gliding along the rails at sixty miles an hour with our private room and bed, a man-sized bar and restaurant stocked with celebrities in two of the cars, and smiling waiters and porters appearing at the ring of the bell. We were neatly insulated from everything beyond the railroad's right of way and even beyond our own track through the 1930s.

We stayed in Chicago for a few days renewing some of the friendships that I'd built during my growing-up years, then we continued following our trunks onto the Canadian Pacific and eventually wound slowly through the Canadian Rockies, which became and stayed the most beautiful sight of the entire trip.

Maybe I was viewing it all through the light heart of Eleanor Twitchell, the new Gehrig; but I've flown over the Rockies many times since then and I still remember nothing to compare with that meandering course of two days on the rails. The train took the most scenic part very slowly, and you could ignore the highball in your hand while drinking in the extravagant scenery. Trout jumping in the streams along the tracks, the train actually stopping at a tiny boarding station while the trainmen hauled some fish aboard for dinner. Then we burst into a clearing and suddenly faced the spectacular resort hotel on Lake Louise.

That's where we wanted to stop the world and get off, but we went straight through to Vancouver and directly to the ship. It was the night before sailing, and ballplayers were arriving from all parts of the country with their wives to be piped aboard by Mr. Mack. I don't suppose that Connie Mack ever asked to be addressed as "Mr. Mack," and it had nothing to do with the fact that his real name was Cornelius McGillicuddy. It probably had nothing to do with his age, either, though he already was as

---

It was a test of will, I suppose, because Colonel Ruppert was offering $39,000—and the price stayed there for weeks. In fact, Lou missed the entire spring-training season because of the deadlock. But he finally surrendered for $39,000, and that was the highest salary he ever commanded in his baseball career.

There I was, Twitchell of Chicago, the wild-and-woolly and toddlin'
town, riding through life as Mrs. Lou, the baseball wife. . . . We had
planned on his retiring from baseball when he reached thirty-five, even
if he was still doing terrifically well by then. So we made our pact.

188

spare and white-haired as a prophet. He just stood out, tall and erect and dignified; when you sat in his quarters on the ship listening to his stories about errant heroes like his old pitching prodigy Rube Waddell, you would start to say something in reply and it always came out "Mr. Mack."

So there I was, one year away from my "own" life in Chicago and one year into a new life with my Luke and the people who filled his world. Overjoyed, almost gloating that we were embarked not only on a memorable trip to the faraway places on maps and inside travel folders but also on a memorable trip through faraway years. Without fear, without even concern, without anybody's crystal ball to help us peer into the future; without any need to peer beyond the next anecdote or inning or loud laugh.

Highs or lows, they were all new to us, and they were all staffed with intriguing people. Sometimes the "highs" involved little nuances of shipboard manners—the captain's inviting us to cocktails every night and appointing me as his official hostess. Sometimes the "lows" involved little nuances of palace politics that created an "episode" in our personal logbook.

The principal episode started innocently enough one day when I was walking the deck alone, a calm day in a fairly rough crossing, and I passed Claire Ruth, who was sitting in a deck chair. We both said "hello" spontaneously. I kept walking, but on the way back she invited me

He had played in 2,130 baseball games in a row. My Iron Man. . . .
(Culver Pictures, Inc.)

to their cabin, where I stepped into *their* little world: the resplendent Babe, sitting like a Buddha figure, cross-legged and surrounded by an empire of caviar and champagne. It was an extravagant picnic, especially since I'd never been able to get my fill of caviar, and suddenly I was looking up at mounds of it.

So I was "missing" for two hours, the longest that I'd been out of Lou's sight since the trip began. When I finally stepped back outside into the rest of the world's problems, I found Lou and most of the crew in a stem-to-stern search on the brink of blasting the ship's horn for a circling hunt for a body overboard. I'd been "overboard," all right, but the one place Lou had never thought to check out was Babe Ruth's cabin.

The result was a long siege of no-speaking, one of Lou's spells of speechlessness, and we were silently dressing for dinner later when there was a muscular banging on the door. Babe Ruth burst in—jovial, arms both stretched out in a let's-be-pals gesture. But my unforgiving man turned his back, extending the silent treatment to the party of the second part, and the Babe retreated. They never did become reconciled, and I just dropped the subject forever.

Their feud, their ridiculous new feud, didn't diminish the team's performance when it came to baseball; we simply went our separate ways, the Ruths and the Gehrigs. Ruth was on his way out as a player anyway, and during the next season he was destined to land in a Boston Braves uniform as a sort of co-manager, part-time player and full-time attraction after a historic generation as the big man of the Yankees. It was silly, it was sad, that their final "road trip" of any consequence should be queered by champagne, caviar and bruised feelings. But it was, and that was life in the showcase, too.

After we'd reached Yokohama, the port city and the ocean gateway to Honshu, we transferred to a train for Tokyo. *That* turned out to be an upset, too, because the crowd that greeted us was immense. It stretched from here to there, as far as the eye could see. No pushing or shoving, just polite calls and shouts, and offerings of chrysanthemums that were draped around our necks—and that were replenished all the while we stayed in Japan.

On the train ride into Tokyo, we began to notice the population problem, and it didn't have much to do with the size of the welcoming throngs. Every inch of ground was under cultivation right up to the tracks, and the farmers and their wives were bending knee-deep in the rice paddies, with the women often carting their babies strapped papoose-style to their backs.

When we reached Tokyo half an hour later, the crowd was even thicker, as were the chrysanthemums. What we noticed there, though, was that many persons in the swarm wore white masks over their noses and mouths. For a time, I wondered if there had been an outbreak of some kind, but we were told that this was a protection against smog, and this was back in 1934. Some people wore face masks when they had colds, sort of a civic hygiene, but the main thing was the smog. All the way to the Imperial Hotel, the streets were packed with spectators, half the women in kimonos, the rest in modern dress.

This was a pretty good bunch of American ballplayers,

the "elite" of the business back home, but this was one of the early trips abroad by touring professional athletes. Now, a generation or two later, the "tour" is more commonplace. *Any* travel is more commonplace, for that matter, especially since the global switching around made necessary by World War II and later made possible by the jet airplane. But when we unpacked in the Imperial Hotel, it was still a novelty, and so were we.

The Japanese took their sports passionately and they took our heroes in "their" sports just as passionately. Baseball ruled the roost there, and still does, even in these days of runaway competition for the public's mind and purse. Every bank clerk and messenger boy played the game in Japan, every road leading to the public parks was clogged with bicycle traffic carying sandlot players to their battle stations (even early in the morning, not long after dawn). It was almost as though all the barnstorming trips back home had been hammered into one gigantic tour, with Babe Ruth and Lou Gehrig and Jimmie Foxx playing the lead roles.

Our permanent base of operations was the hotel, but we also took side visits to Kyoto, Hiroshima, Nagasaki, Nagoya and other cities that a few years later would become entries in the history books. We received a list of "appointments" every day that was overwhelming, and we received an official line of limousines in front of the hotel every day that also seemed overwhelming. Oh yes, somehow a ball game had to be played every afternoon, too, and that could be overwhelming in its own way as well.

Take the opening game as a "for instance." The Tokyo

Stadium was huge, but every seat had been sold and the turnout was colossal, as though the Yankees were fighting the Boston Red Sox on the Fourth of July in one of those holiday doubleheaders.

Before the game, both teams marched around the field like circus stars. Then the Japanese in the line of march paused and bowed before an empty box—the emperor's box, and even though the emperor never attended any game at any time, they bowed respectfully in the direction of the box anyway. We noticed that they also bowed whenever they happened to pass the Imperial Palace. In those days, the emperor rarely left the grounds, if ever, and he was considered a sort of celestial being.

Once the game started, we traveling wives were arrayed in one section behind the dugout while our men toyed with the home team like titans taking their exercise. But we noticed that the stands, though packed with people, stayed strangely silent. No booing or yelling or cheering, and they didn't even heckle the umpires, which was strange in itself to our nomads who had grown up on "raspberries" in the ball park. A sharp fielding play on either side was rewarded by polite hand-clapping, and that was just about all the outward reaction. The Japanese players tended to be small men (though later they ranged in size more or less the way American players do), and the home runs that began to disappear into the right-field bleachers caused a flurry of excitement—even a few gasps—but no more than another round of hand-clapping and wide-eyed attention from the crowd. Ebbets Field and Yankee Stadium were never like this.

For that matter, they didn't even clamor around our heroes for autographs. Instead, they propped themselves in the hotel corridors and spent the night waiting for our players to awaken in the morning. Then the hotel-room doors would open for room service, and that became the signal for the incredibly patient vigil-keepers to make their moves. They would step forward, offer some small gift as a token of esteem, and then shyly extend a piece of paper or a baseball to be signed. No, Ebbetts Field was never like that, either.

For a baseball bride like myself, maybe the most enduring sights were on the streets and in the restaurants. The Japanese are devoted hosts, but they usually do not bring their wives to social events; at least, not in those days they didn't. I'm told that Women's Lib is making some inroads into the structure of society there today, but we used to watch in some wonder while the wives followed the husbands around, a few feet to the rear, at a respectful distance. We seldom saw a man and woman strolling together, and never saw them kissing or making any great sign of emotion that would be considered commonplace back in the States. This was also before television brought love into the living-rooms of either Japan *or* America.

We also found that walking down the Ginza was like walking down Broadway, with record shops blaring away but with no hookers. They were segregated in a big section of town called the Ishawara, and their photos were posted outside individual huts with a pimp giving a spiel and literally selling tickets, but your time inside the hut was strictly limited, as though you were buying a ticket for the roller coaster.

We also walked past clusters of "sex stores," the kind that became fixtures much later in Times Square or in the center of many cities back home. All sorts of fancy ticklers, colorful gadgets, miraculous "get strong" salves. We weren't too shocked by it all, but it did seem kind of funny parading through this section behind the tall, spare and absolutely dignified figure of Mr. Mack, who saw no evil, spoke no evil and heard no evil.

We didn't do much shopping in Japan because we were scheduled to stop in Shanghai and Hong Kong afterwards, and we had been advised to wait until we got there for the "real" bargains. But I bought several pieces of matchless *satsuma* ware that was compared to the French *cloisonné*. We were loaded down with gifts, though, so shopping sprees weren't exactly required. Everywhere we went, we were given kimonos; each of us received a complete dinner set of twelve settings from the leading manufacturer of china ware; and fine jade was all over the place.

But my most enduring memory came one day when the ballplayers were taken to one of the northern cities for a game and the wives stayed behind in Tokyo. It was just for a day, but my day was "made" there, 7,000 miles from home, when they delivered a telegram to me. Small and square and short: "I miss you today, I love you." My man Luke.

The baseball team that toured Japan in 1934 could be the best one ever put together. There were Lou and Lefty Gomez and Ruth from the Yankees, though they had just released Babe after fifteen seasons; Charlie Gehringer of the Detroit Tigers, Earl Averill of the Cleveland Indians along with Clint Brown and Moe Berg, who was a linguist and sort of roving scout for the government (spelled "spy," we were told years later); Earl Whitehill of the Washington Senators, and a whole bunch from Mr. Mack's Philadelphia Athletics—Foxx, Eric McNair, Frank Hayes, Joe Cascarella and Ed Miller.

All our expenses were paid, and there was enough money left over for sizable bonuses, besides. So Lou and I decided to just keep on traveling after the series of ball games in Japan. And after the team had disbanded, we set sail to the west and went home by way of "the rest of the world."

We spent only a few days in each port, but we lived it up wherever we went. At Singapore, we went ashore *armed*, victims of our own imaginations and a lot of "B" movies we'd seen. So, instead of falling victim there to Oriental conspiracies, we fell victim to the English colonials who were in Singapore in those days. They escorted us to their tropical racetrack and the lush golf club that was combined with it. We even dropped into a movie house where the local folks were howling at the cutups of Shirley Temple in *Little Miss Marker*.

When we disembarked at Bombay, though, we were in another world. No racetrack palaces or happy talk, just hordes of disfigured beggars—and babies everywhere. We were shocked at the overpopulation of all the large cities of the Far East and the rest of Asia. We found that walking was hazardous at night in Bombay, partly because you had to step over or around people who had fallen asleep on the sidewalks, or dropped on them. In the daytime, vultures circled overhead; and we got our final dose of repellent when we decided to visit the Taj Mahal and were advised to take our own bedding for the train trip. We were young, we were cheerfully married, we were even honeymooning our way around the globe—but we were getting a fresh taste of the bitterness that besieged much of the world outside our own insulated little home back in New York.

In Cairo, we took a taxi out to the Pyramids and received another education. A lot of the bedraggled men there claimed to be "sheiks," but their only resemblance to Rudolph Valentino's brand of sheik was the turban they wore. We also rented a pair of camels from the concession where the taxis left us, and we got ourselves photographed aboard; but that time we learned that camel lice are very persistent creatures with a pest-span of about one week.

Then on to Naples and Rome and the "Western world." We loved Rome above all the cities we visited, even though I found that some of the men showed their appreciation of the women by pinching—sometimes in full dress at the opera house. I say that I "found" this custom to be flourishing; but maybe it would be more accurate (certainly more politic) to say that I "observed" it.

In Munich, the mood turned dire: Adolf Hitler was making fast headway by then, and it was clear from the conversations Lou was able to carry on with the beer hall crowd that "die Juden" and other minority groups were on the brink of a disastrous time. Pictures of Hitler glared from most of the store windows, and it was no joke whenever the border guards kept examining our passports all the way to Paris. Again, our happy honeymoon was being sobered by life outside our own sphere of baseball crowds and cheering stadiums back home. We were learning the hard way.

We were met in Paris by members of the Paris *Herald Tribune*, the English-language link to New York, and they took us everywhere. Then, by the time we reached London, I was practically bedridden and, in a weary voice, asked Lou to go down to the desk and get me a *New York Times*. Instead, he came back with a real live link to New York: Jimmy Walker and his wife Betty, and we spent the next two days and nights with them, four Americans abroad, living on the edge of the earthquake that was gathering around Europe and the world.

We finally got home in time for Lou to get into a contract hassle with Colonel Ruppert, his most serious and his longest holdout. Today an arbitrator is asked to decide if a baseball player should get his "price asked" or the "price bid" by the management. But in those days, before players came to the bargaining table with lawyers or agents, it was you against the boss. In this case, Colonel Ruppert simply wouldn't go for Lou's price, which was $40,000. It was a test of will, I suppose, because Ruppert was offering $39,000—and the price stayed there for weeks. Lou missed the entire spring-training season because of the deadlock. But he finally surrendered for $39,000, and that was the highest salary Lou ever commanded in his baseball career.

But he came through the experience disheartened, something like we came through the stark parts of our sightseeing. He was over thirty now, he had played in eight World Series, he had shared in the winner's purse seven of the eight times. But more and more, he was becoming thoughtful about his future outside baseball and he was still determined to quit on his thirty-fifth birthday, no matter how well he was playing then. Not that he ever looked down on baseball, but every once in a while he got the feeling that he was only playing a game in the scheme of things. His horizons were widening—literally on our long trip and figuratively in many other ways—and he was beginning to get offers from friends and promoters.

Some of the offers were interesting, some were ridiculous. But they were growing stronger in his thinking, and so was his fixation about calling it quits when he turned the magic number: thirty-five. The date would be June 19, 1939. A date to remember.

Whenever I get the feeling that I was too close to things to remember them objectively, I reach for other people's memories. Like Paul Gallico's:

"And so they were married and lived happily ever after. Or at least, they lived happily, because the shadow of their tragedy was not yet over them. Lou, who had never known much gaiety or frivolity, began to learn to enjoy life.

"Up at 10 in the morning for a large breakfast, or brunch, since he would not eat again until evening. Three or four eggs with bacon or ham, sausages on the side, with wheatcakes, toast, fruit and coffee. He left for the ball park at noon so as to be there for batting practice, which started at 1 P.M. Usually Eleanor went with him. The game would be over around 5 in the afternoon, when they would drive home. They rarely went out to dinner during the season. Lou liked to eat at home and, more, he liked to be in Eleanor's company. He liked people, but he seemed to be jealous once he was married, jealous of every moment that deprived him of the company of his girl. He had been so long finding her.

"But for the flavor of the marriage, you must come into their home and see this big guy with the loud voice, the bright, friendly eyes and the dimples at the corners of his mouth, stamping into the house like a half-tamed earthquake and yelling for his dinner. . . . He'd call for his Eleanor with a howl of 'Where's the old bat? Hey, Hag, come out here and fight like a man.'

"To him, she was the old bat, the old bitch, the bag and the battle-axe, but when people were around he called her 'Pal' or 'my pal.' He was always 'Lou' to her, except in the more earnest moments of baiting one another when he became The Monster, Dracula or Frankenstein. When he traveled, he would always get off the train at Harmon and she would drive over from Larchmont and pick him up. It was a never-failing ritual.

"Once when he arrived, the car was there with a chauffeur, but no Eleanor. Lou was furious. He burned to a crisp. Then he grew morose. It was obvious that Eleanor didn't love him anymore, otherwise she wouldn't have forgotten him to play bridge or gab with females. He got into the car. Two miles down the road, two outlandish-looking females with long red noses and Victorian costumes stood by the side of the road, thumbing Lou's car for a ride. When the chauffeur stopped, they piled in and all over Lou. It was Eleanor and a girl friend."

True enough, I guess; at least, the quality was true enough. The rollicking times were there, the horseplay, the feeling that we were a long way from Bombay or Munich, and relishing every minute of it. Even when Lou occasionally would get bogged down by some physical problem and people would start to worry about the legend that was growing along with his so-called endurance streak, which passed 1,250 during the 1933 season and stretched on past 1,550 midway through the 1935 season. That was *games in a row*, and his closest call came during the summer before our trip to Japan when Lou singled in the second inning against the Tigers in Detroit, ran to first base and suddenly doubled over.

He nearly fell down but managed to reach the bag, then found that he couldn't straighten up. So Earle Combs, who was coaching at first base, called time and asked if he'd pulled a muscle.

"No," Lou said, shaking his head and wincing, "I think I must have caught cold in my back. It bothered me a little bit last night and again this morning, but this is the first I've felt it since I came out to the park."

By then, they had been joined by Art Fletcher from the coaching box at third base and Joe McCarthy from the dugout, and Combs was still trying to laugh it off by saying: "A cold in his back or something. Maybe lumbago. You're getting old, Lou."

He stayed in the game and Ben Chapman followed with a single to right field, sending Lou to second—but barely to second. Then Bill Dickey pulled a line drive to Jo Jo White in center field and Lou, who had headed for third, couldn't reverse directions on time and was doubled off second on White's throw in to Billy Rogell, the shortstop.

In the home half of the inning, Lou signaled that he was through, so he went inside and flopped on Doc Painter's training table in the clubhouse. He stayed there, too, long after everybody else had gone back to the hotel after the game—while Painter applied heat treatments and massage. Lou was awake with the pain most of the night, finally dropping off to sleep around dawn. But he struggled into his clothes that morning, went back out to the ball park and tried to take batting practice. No soap.

That's when he asked McCarthy for a little help in keeping his streak alive.

"Since Frank Crosetti leads off," he suggested, "put me in the batting order as shortstop and I'll take one time at bat, so that the record will show that I actually played in the game. Then I'll go out and Frankie will take his usual place, okay?"

McCarthy said okay, then discovered that Crosetti wasn't feeling so well, either. So he assigned Red Rolfe to play shortstop once Lou had left the game. Anyway, Lou crunched his way up to the plate as the lead-off hitter in the game, couldn't take a full swing at the ball because of the pain, sort of lunged at it with his bat, got a piece of the ball and singled to right field. He managed to jog down to first base, ninety aching feet away, touched the bag and then headed back to Doc Painter's table inside. The next day, he returned to the lineup at first base, and most people forgot about the incident. But James M. Kahn, who didn't forget, wrote in the *New York Post:* "This was Gehrig's closest escape from having his endurance mark broken, and it is given in detail because it may hold an additional interest for medical men. These attacks occurred occasionally and escaped accurate diagnosis, invariably doubling him over and making it painful and difficult for him to breathe until they wore off in a couple of days. For convenience in reporting them and because of the absence of anything more definite, the sportswriters referred to the attacks as lumbago. Gehrig became quite sensitive to the curiosity of the reporters after a while when these attacks hit him, which they did three or four times over a period of four or five years."

He had gone to bat 579 times in 1934, got 210 hits, 49 home runs, 165 runs batted in—and finished with an average of .363. A year later, despite the time lost in his salary wrangle with Ruppert, he went to bat 535 times, made 176 hits that included 30 home runs, knocked in 119 runs and hit .329. And by then, Babe Ruth was gone from the Yankee scene and Lou was one of the last links to the power teams of the twenties.

In 1936, Joe DiMaggio arrived from San Francisco of the Pacific Coast League and the Yankees began another phase of their long reign, taking the first of four straight pennants and World Series. Lou hit .354 with 49 home runs, batted in 152 runs and was again voted the Most Valuable Player in the league. A year later, more of the same: a .351 average with 37 home runs and 159 runs batted in.

It was the last time he would hit .300, but we didn't realize it then. He was still playing every day, and most days was playing every inning, in spite of the occasional sieges of lumbago or whatever it was. He was also nearing his thirty-fifth birthday, but we were too busy and too happy to worry about that. Too caught up to worry yet that he was only playing a game in the scheme of things.

12

The Luckiest Man

"WHAT'S the difference between a baseball player in the high minor leagues and a man in the major leagues?" I asked one day when we got to talking about weighty, far-away things like retiring. And Lou Gehrig looked straight at me and said: "One step."

He had been the regular first baseman for the Yankees since June 1, 1925, and now it was 1938 and Lou still hadn't "lost" that one step. Not so's you'd notice, anyway. He did admit to me privately that his legs didn't feel so strong or springy, and they hadn't since he turned thirty. He was losing *something*—like fifty-six points in his batting average. But he was surrounded by swarms of new Yankees like Joe DiMaggio, who would play center field for fifteen years, and Joe Gordon, who replaced Tony Lazzeri at second base, while the team rolled along without losing any collective steps. And every day when he jogged out to first base, Luke added another game to his own strange record for playing without a break.

It was strange because there was no particular reason to keep playing without a break, no particular compulsion—except the fascination to add one more day, one more week, whatever you lost.

Then he reached 1,999 games in a row early in the season of 1938, and the fascination bit *me*. But it was the fascination to shatter the spell, not to stay wrapped in it; to take charge of your own "thing" before it took charge of you. So when he dressed that morning to drive down to the stadium for No. 2,000, there I was—thinking about the unthinkable.

"Lou," I said, firing from the hip, "I've got an idea. *Don't* go to the stadium today. Tell them anything you want, but skip it."

"Skip it?" he said, sort of shocked at the thought, almost as though it were a sacrilege. "You know I can't just skip it. They've got a ceremony planned and things like that, and Ruppert would be wild."

"So what?" Twitchell went on, baiting the hook. "Look, if you're worried about the streak, think how they'll remember a streak that stopped at 1,999 games in a row. That's a lot more memorable than 2,000. It'll make a terrific splash, much more than if you show up and go through the motions. 'Gehrig Stops at 1,999'—you can see the headlines now. Besides, let's just do it for the sake of doing it ourselves. We can stay home and drink champagne."

He was intrigued and appalled, but more appalled than intrigued, so he shook loose of my clutches and got out of there before I cast a reverse spell of my own. "I couldn't," he said, caught between two compulsions but finally escaping mine and heading spellbound in the direction of his own.

"All they'll do is hang a horseshoe of flowers around your neck," I said, firing a parting shot. But he went, out the door of the house and into the door of Yankee Stadium, drawn toward the magnet generated by that nice round row of zeroes in the numerals that said Gehrig had somehow made the lineup for 2,000 games without sitting one out, and drawn by the conventional hoopla that the zeros would generate. And so I sat there, proud of it, afraid of it, craving the chance for us to cut the "chain that binds me fast." But chained we were.

Six hours later, the door was nudged open a crack, and my Iron Man lurked across the threshold like a truant. There was a long pause, then the door opened wider and there he stood—a sheepish grin on his square face, a huge horseshoe of flowers hung around his neck.

Then the place exploded. I charged him, hugged him, wrestled him and the horseshoe of flowers to the floor, pounded him, got pounded in return, tearing at him and the blossoms both, laughing and shrieking and crying. And we dissolved into the champagne, glass after glass, toast after toast for the whole glorious evening, plucking the flowers off the framework one by one and pelting each

other with them, his dream of "2,000" come true, my sar-
castic prediction of a horseshoe of flowers come true. Pelting each other, pelting the house with flowers, pelting the
tyrant in our life that they represented.

But there was another tyrant creeping into our life besides the tyrant of public conformity—much more private,
much less visible, incredibly more demanding. I wasn't
nearly so sharp in spotting it, either, as I'd been in visual-
izing the inevitable horseshoe of carnations. Nor did I
prove so calculating in attacking it as I'd been in disman-
tling the blooming flowers.

With an athlete like Lou, especially with one who makes
headlines with his muscles and who flexes them in public
for thirteen straight years, nobody blows a whistle and
says gently: "You've had it, lad. You may make a graceful
exit now, or you may stumble out the door a little later."
Too many sidelights and side issues and side personalities
confuse the problem. Too many memories and hopes
flood to your defense, promising great expectations and
delivering small clues that feed your fantasies or that
slowly dilute them.

In his case, the chief distraction was probably the fact
that he was surrounded by strong young Yankees who in
turn were surrounded by continuing success. They were
steered along in 1938 by Joe McCarthy, a manager who
supposedly turned on the baseball machine in April and in
a vague and precise way simply watched it operate on all
cylinders until October. Joe DiMaggio in center field,
flanked by George Selkirk and Tommy Henrich. Bill
Dickey doing the catching without flaws and giving the

signs to pitchers like Red Ruffing, Lefty Gomez, Spud Chandler, Bump Hadley, Monte Pearson, Steve Sundra and Johnny Murphy. A relentlessly coordinated infield with Red Rolfe at third base, Frank Crosetti at shortstop, Joe Gordon at second—and Gehrig at first, the Iron Man anchoring it all.

He batted only .295 that summer, and it was the first time he had slipped below the magic mark of .300 in a dozen summers. He hit 29 home runs, and it was his smallest power production in ten summers. He knocked in 114 runs, and that was the fewest for him since 1926. But the Yankees kept winning, bowling along toward that third pennant and World Series in a row, so Gehrig's "slump" was measured chiefly in contrast to his own high performance of the seasons past. To many people, he was just paying the price of all that durability.

"I think there's something wrong with him," Jim Kahn said, offering one sportswriter's dissent to the babble of guessing. "Physically wrong, I mean. I don't know what it is. But I am satisfied that it goes far beyond his ball-playing. I have seen ballplayers 'go' overnight, as Gehrig seems to have done. But they were simply washed up as ballplayers. It's something deeper than that in this case, though.

"I have watched him very closely and this is what I have seen: I have seen him time a ball perfectly, swing on it as hard as he can, meet it squarely—and drive a soft, looping fly over the infield. In other words, for some reason that I do not know, his old power isn't there. He isn't popping the ball into the air or hitting it into the dirt or striking out. He is meeting the ball, time after time, and it isn't going anywhere."

But Jim Kahn's analysis did not rock the boat as the Yankees sailed serenely to their pennant and, in the World Series that fall, they overpowered the Chicago Cubs in four straight games and became the first baseball club in history to win three World Series in a row. Lou, who once hit .545 in a World Series and .529 in another, managed to hit .286 in this one: 4 hits in 14 times at bat. But he made no doubles, no triples and no home runs. His 4 hits were looping singles, and somewhere in the creeping mystery of that summer he had lost the power of a man who had hit 494 baseballs over fences while playing in 2,122 games in a row.

He accepted a $3,000 cut in salary, the first time in his career that he had accepted a cut, and then he joined the guessing, too: "I tired in midseason. I don't know why, but I just couldn't get going again."

"Do you think you have overdone it by playing every day?" he was asked, time after time.

And, time after time, he would answer with one word: "No." When he was reminded that Babe Ruth had suggested a "few days off for fishing" if the strain started wearing him down, he would head it off by saying: "Well, the strain hasn't got me yet."

Do you have any doubts about yourself for 1939?

"None at all. Why should I? I just had a bad year last year."

But long before his teammates and the public notice, an athlete detects signals that he is beginning to slip. It begins ever so slightly in the legs: He still gets the hits, but he *knows*. And Lou, despite his curt words, despite his rationalizing, began to detect that something was slipping from his control. His arms were weakening and his coordination was off, too. So he took the first step—to a specialist for a checkup—and came away with a tentative diagnosis: His gallbladder was upset. He was put on a bland diet, headed south for spring training in 1939, did some fishing off Key Largo, reported to St. Pete—and got a little weaker.

He responded the way you'd expect: by driving himself harder, as though he could rebuild the tension in all those muscles. In our hotel, he did exercises; at Huggins Field, he circled the track extra times like a hungry rookie. But most people just looked the other way, afraid to confront him or his problem. Then I drove the car north from Florida to New York while the Yankees played their way home, finally arriving for their weekend exhibition series against the Brooklyn Dodgers before opening the rush for pennant No. 4.

Frank Graham, one of the writers who followed the team, remembered that Lou hit two singles and two home runs against the Dodgers in Norfolk in the last of the barnstorming games en route north. Then, on the gray and cold afternoon when they played the Dodgers in Ebbets Field, a reporter who had not gone south for spring training buttonholed McCarthy as the manager sat in the dugout, his hands shoved into the pockets of his blue windbreaker.

"How's DiMaggio?" the writer asked. "How's Gordon? How's Gomez?"

"All right," McCarthy replied in his low key. "All right. DiMaggio looks great. This is the first time we've had him through the whole training season. No accidents this time."

He tapped for luck on the wooden bench. Then the reporter waited a bit and asked: "How's Gehrig?"

McCarthy shook his head, was reminded that Lou had hit two singles and two home runs in Norfolk and finally said: "The singles were all right. The home runs were fly balls over a short right-field fence."

The Yankees took the field for infield practice. Everybody watched Lou laboring around first base, and the writer turned to McCarthy and said: "He looks worse than I thought he would. What's the matter with him?"

And Joe McCarthy said: "I don't know."

But McCarthy chose to look the other way, too, and he opened the season with Gehrig at first base as usual, though without his usual drive. In Washington, in the eighth game of the new season, they lost by one run and by now not everybody was looking the other way. As Lou sloughed into the locker room at Griffith Stadium, he heard somebody say: "Why doesn't he quit? He's through. We can't win with him in there."

He hesitated a moment outside, got his composure back, then came into view inside the clubhouse. Then everybody stopped talking at once, and he dressed in absolute silence.

The Yankees took the train back to New York for an off-day at home before moving on to Detroit for their first western swing, and when I met him at the door he was a

changed man: troubled, shaken, even shocked. He told me
what had happened, so we stayed up half the night and
talked, and talked some more.

"They don't think I can do it anymore," he said.
"Maybe I can, maybe I can't. But they're talking about it
now, they're even writing about it. And when they're not
talking, I can almost feel what they're thinking. Then, I
wish to God that they would talk—you know, say anything but sit there looking."

"Sweetheart, you've done it for thirteen years without a
day off," I told him. "The only thing that matters is
whether you get the same feeling of satisfaction out of it."

"How can I get the same feeling of satisfaction out of
it?" he asked. "I'm not giving them the same thing, so I'm
not getting the same thing. You think they're hurting me.
But I'm hurting *them*, that's the difference."

How do you put it? Where do you find the words to say
it? I finally reminded him that he'd always said he would
step down as soon as he felt he could no longer help the
Yankees on the field. Then, gently, probably devasta-
tingly, I told him the heartbreaking words: "Maybe that
time's come."

McCarthy had gone home to Buffalo for that day off,
but when he reached Detroit the next morning, Lou was
waiting for him in the lobby of the hotel. He followed Joe
up to his room, waited for the bellhop to leave, then said:
"I'm benching myself, Joe."

The only thing McCarthy could manage to say at a
moment he had dreaded as much as Lou was: "Why?"

"For the good of the team," Lou said, not meaning to

sound just noble or sacrificing. "I can't tell you how grateful I am for the kindness you've shown me and for your patience. I've tried hard, you know that. But I just can't seem to get going, and nobody has to tell me how bad I've been. I've been thinking, ever since the season opened— when I saw that I couldn't start as I'd hoped—that the time had come for me to quit."

"All right, Lou," McCarthy said. "Take a rest. I'll put Babe Dahlgren on first base. But I want you to know that that's your position—and whenever you want it back, all you have to do is walk out there and take it."

It was May 2, 1939, and for the first time since June 1, 1925, the Yankees took the field that afternoon without Gehrig. He sat in the dugout, alone with his thoughts, after 2,130 baseball games.

He stayed with the team, but didn't play again. He would usually stay out of sight until game-time, then McCarthy would send him up to home plate to present the lineup card to the umpires and to hear the standing ovation for that symbolic bit of work for the Yankees. They headed back to New York by way of Philadelphia and I went down to join them and, for the first time, I saw a Yankee game without Gehrig, too. I saw him walk to the plate with McCarthy's lineup card and I saw old Connie Mack come hurrying out of the Philadelphia dugout, tall and straight and wearing that old-fashioned suit of his with the starched white collar. Mr. Mack had long since delegated *his* role in the lineup ceremony to his son, but this time he strode across the grass with his hand extended

and shook hands with my sad, sick Luke while the crowd
stood and cheered.

A month later, more like a lifetime later, I made my
telephone call from the upstairs room of the 21 Club in
New York—the call to the Mayo Clinic. That evening,
from our home in Larchmont, I made the other call—to
Lou in the Del Prado Hotel in Chicago. The next morning, he flew to Rochester, Minnesota, and six days later
Dr. Mayo and Dr. O'Leary telephoned me with the ver-
dict: amyotrophic lateral sclerosis. It was June 19, Lou's
thirty-sixth birthday, and they were telling me that he had
maybe two and a half years to live.

Now it is July 4, and they are having something called
"Lou Gehrig Appreciation Day" in Yankee Stadium. The
Yankees are playing a doubleheader against the Washington Senators, the way big-league teams always used to
play those holiday doubleheaders, and the place is filled.
All the old Yankees are back, too: Bob Meusel, Herb Pennock, Waite Hoyt, Joe Dugan, Mark Koenig, Benny
Bengough, Tony Lazzeri, Earle Combs and Bob Shawkey
from the no-nonsense teams of the 1920s, the "early dy-
nasty." And Wally Pipp, who decided to skip that game in
1925, giving Lou his shot at the lineup. And Everett
Scott, who played in 1,307 straight games, a record that
Lou passed and broke by 823 games—or, to put it another
way, by nearly *six years*.

Then, after the first game of the doubleheader was over,
they set up a microphone at home plate and everybody

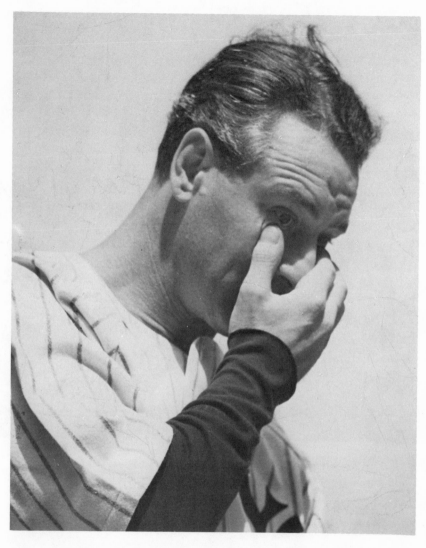

July 4, 1939: "Yet today I consider myself the luckiest man on the face of the earth. . . ."

Mayor LaGuardia was a courtly little man who waved away the fussy details of things, and he waved away the details this time. He simply gave Lou a ten-year appointment as one of the city's three Commissioners of Parole. I worked out a side deal with the mayor—I would tell him when Lou's judgment or strength began to wane. (Wide World Photos, Inc.)

Sometimes the prisoners would complain to him that "I got a bad break." He would just be silent for a moment and let the complaint hang there in the air: *bad break*. (Wide World Photos, Inc.)

stood around—the 1927 Yankees and the others, Fiorello LaGuardia, James A. Farley, the baseball writers and even Babe Ruth, big and bear-like, arriving late and throwing his arms around Lou's neck and hugging away the feuds of the past summers.

They hauled out a dazzling bunch of gifts from everybody whose working world had touched Lou's working world for the better part of a generation: the Yankees, the Giants, the Harry M. Stevens catering family, the newspaper men, the stadium ushers, the ticket-sellers, the clerks, the men on the turnstiles, the ground crew, the Babe. The Yankees' token was a silver trophy with an engraved poem that had been written by John Kieran of the *Times*, saying:

> We've been to the wars together,
> We took our foes as they came;
> And always you were the leader,
> And ever you played the game.
>
> Idol of cheering millions;
> Records are yours by sheaves;
> Iron of frame they hailed you,
> Decked you with laurel leaves.
>
> But higher than that we hold you,
> We who have known you best;
> Knowing the way you came through
> Every human test.
>
> Let this be a silent token
> Of lasting friendship's gleam
> And all that we've left unspoken
> —Your Pals on the Yankee Team.

Then I watched my Luke walking to the microphone in his pinstriped uniform, the "home" uniform in white with the big No. 4 on the broad back of the shirt. He glanced briefly at the 70,000 or so people, who were all standing now, and he replied to it all with the mixed feelings of the class valedictorian, trying to sum up things in words before moving into whatever waited "beyond."

He had written it down, but hadn't rehearsed it, probably because it was simple enough and agonizing enough and he was still shy enough, groping for some way to phrase the emotions that usually were kept securely locked up. Later they called it his "farewell speech," though few knew what he was saying farewell to; few in the stadium in the Bronx who listened silently as he spoke from memory over the public-address system and few who listened over the radio. Tallulah Bankhead was listening downtown in her dressing room at the theater, radio engineers were listening in their control rooms, sun-worshippers were listening on portable radio sets at the Fourth of July beaches, and I was listening a few feet away. This is the way it came out of the microphone standing at home plate, where he had stood 13,888 times with a bat in his hands:

"Fans, for the past two weeks you have been reading about a bad break I got. Yet today I consider myself the luckiest man on the face of the earth. I have been in ball parks for 17 years, and have never received anything but kindness and encouragement from you fans.

"Look at these grand men. Which of you wouldn't consider it the highlight of his career just to associate with them for even one day?

"Sure I'm lucky. Who wouldn't consider it an honor to have known Jacob Ruppert; also the builder of baseball's greatest empire, Ed Barrow; to have spent six years with that wonderful little fellow, Miller Huggins; then to have spent the next nine years with that outstanding leader, that smart student of psychology—the best manager in baseball today, Joe McCarthy?

"Sure, I'm lucky. When the New York Giants, a team you would give your right arm to beat, and vice versa, sends you a gift—that's something! When everybody down to the groundskeepers and those boys in white coats remember you with trophies—that's something.

"When you have a wonderful mother-in-law who takes sides with you in squabbles against her own daughter—that's something. When you have a father and mother who work all their lives so that you can have an education and build your body—it's a blessing! When you have a wife who has been a tower of strength, and shown more courage than you dreamed existed—that's the finest I know.

"So I close in saying that I might have had a tough break; but I have an awful lot to live for."

He stepped back, brushing his hand across his eyes, perhaps realizing that he had delivered his own requiem—perhaps not. But at least he realized that he had delivered his own farewell to the place he'd gone to work all of his adult life, the men he had worked with, the scenes, the noises, the cheers and challenges. Gone now, fading from his memory while his strength was fading from his body.

So I took him back to our new home in Riverdale, where pheasants roamed the lawns and wild roses bloomed along the driveway and walks, and where our friends and neighbors and the actors and actresses beat their paths to his door. All the entrances to his door could be fitted with ramps, and the inside stairways to the bedrooms could be adapted to a wheelchair, too. But as we settled into our "new" and our last home, I mentioned "wheelchair" only once and drew a withering look in reply. So a wheelchair never rolled into our house during the twenty-three months while we waited inside for the tyrant that had cast this shadow over our life.

Before long, the line of visitors was headed by our neighbor Dr. Esselstyn, the distinguished-looking and imposingly tall man recommended by the Mayo Clinic. He came every morning to "treat" Lou and to help me keep the vigil that began to lock me into the living room downstairs and finally the bedroom upstairs.

My mother was there, too, and we had two servants who did their chores downstairs but who transferred trays of food and other things to my mother. Then she would carry them upstairs to our living quarters, mainly because Lou didn't want anyone to see him as he lost the power from that great sturdy physique and the vitality from that great chiseled face.

Somehow, we had kept Lou's mother at a distance till then. But later I sent two of Lou's friends over to her house in Westchester County along with a doctor from Mayo who'd been attending a convention in New York, and they gently told her that her son was slipping away and that she could visit him when she had composed herself. For once, she entered our house without a chip on her shoulder. She was visiting him for the last time, and I left them alone, no longer worried that she would or could exert the overwhelming influence on his affairs that she had exerted for so long. And she carried it off with something that approached unbelievable grace.

Maybe we all approached grace, or insight, or a kind of perception about life as it faded from him during those months that turned 1939 into 1940 and 1940 into 1941. For the first time in our six, seven, eight years together, there was something I could not discuss with him—the sickness that was draining him gradually until he became helpless—but I still searched the medical books and begged the medical opinion on it until I gradually became steeped in it.

In a healthy person, I found, the nerve fibers are covered with a fatty sheath called myelin, whether the fibers are in the brain, spinal cord or anywhere else in the body. This myelin sheath acts like the insulation on an electric wire. When the disease strikes, a mysterious change occurs that destroys the protective myelin in areas of the nervous system. Mysterious because nobody can answer

Do I have an "answer" to those six years of towering joy followed by those two years of ruin? Do I run the range of feeling and reach bitterness or despair or just anguish? Be honest: Would I trade it all for forty years of lesser joy and lesser tragedy?

"why?" There are some theories that it may be caused by a virus, an allergy, some vitamin deficiency, maybe even a heredity factor.

But whenever the myelin sheath is destroyed, it is replaced by a scar—sclerotic tissue. So wherever the nerve insulation has been damaged, the nerve itself is so affected that impulses no longer pass through. The adjoining parts of the body become paralyzed; the arms and legs often become immobile. And this is what happened to Lou. His hands and arms grew increasingly useless, then his legs could hardly support him; later, speech and even swallowing were impaired.

There is no physical pain in this grim progression. But the actual brain cells remain acutely active, and the patient is only too conscious of the changes taking place in his body. So Lou could almost measure the strength he was losing; but we had told him that he would possibly hit bottom before a change would come, and he waited and watched us, whatever it was that he "knew" in his heart. And that was the greatest pain to me, even after I'd become a clinical expert in amyotrophic lateral sclerosis: the devoted look in his eyes that devoured us—myself, my mother and Dr. "Essy"—with an expression of faith in the three of us. We would bring him through it.

His breathing became more labored, his pulse grew weaker, in the spring of 1941. I stayed by his bedside, occasionally dozing off during those last few weeks. I took

My Luke and I . . .

orange juice and milk shakes, and I often had to look out the window to find out whether it was night or day. The heavy breathing continued, only slower and slower, like a great clock winding down.

Then on the evening of June 2, 1941, suddenly everything was still, and the doctor was by my side. The most beatified expression instantly spread over Lou's face, and I knew the precise moment he had gone.

His expression of peace was beyond description. A thing of ecstatic beauty, and seeing it we were awestricken and even reassured. We didn't cry. We seemed stronger, and not one of us left that room without feeling: There *is* a better place than this. Wherever it is, no tears, no tyrant.

Thirty-five years later, the time passes slowly and more silently. The cheers seemed muffled even when the stadium rocks with noise, when Mrs. Lou Gehrig is introduced and the old Yankees turn toward the front row of boxes, nodding and maybe waving from memory.

Do I have an "answer" to those six years of towering joy followed by those two years of ruin? Do I run the range of feeling and reach bitterness or despair or just anguish? Would I trade it all for forty years of lesser joy and lesser tragedy?

Not ever. Through the summers that have come and gone, there has been no comfort from the thought of basking as a professional widow; and there has been no comfort from the thought of another man, as in his case there could have been no thought of another woman. Loneliness, yes; even emptiness. But I had the "answer," all right.

I would not have traded two minutes of the joy and the grief with that man for two decades of anything with another. Happy or sad, filled with great expectations or great frustrations, we had attained it for whatever brief instant that fate had decided. The most in life, the unattainable, and we were not star-crossed by it. We were blessed with it, my Luke and I.